Highlights™
Hidden Pictures®

Horse Puzzles

HIGHLIGHTS PRESS
Honesdale, Pennsylvania

Welcome, Hidden Pictures® Puzzlers!

When you finish a puzzle, check it off √. Good luck, and happy puzzling!

Contents

Cover art by Mark Corcoran

Come On, Horsey!

leaf

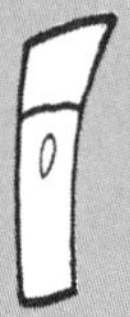

flashlight

hockey stick

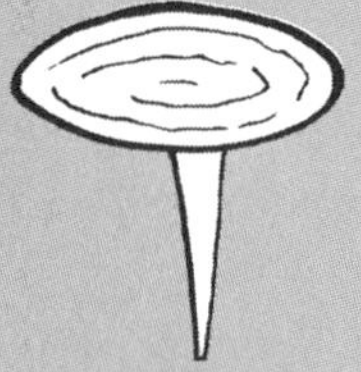

tack

water dipper

boot

needle

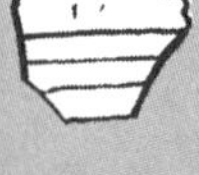

cupcake

toy top

shoe

rocket ship

ice-cream scoop

glove

fish

Art by Chuck Dillon

banana

heart

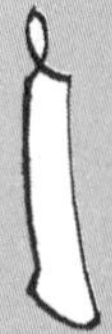
candle

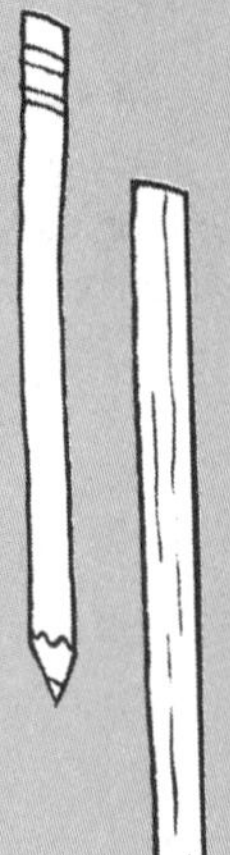
2 pencils

hammer

cowbell

jellyfish

sailboat

bird

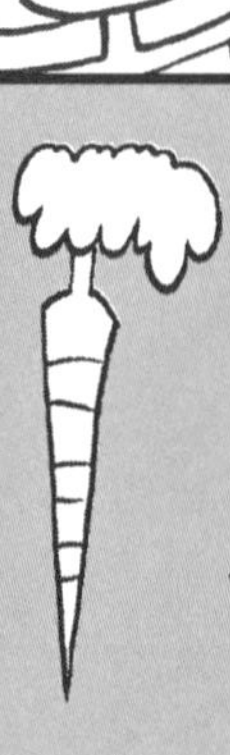
carrot

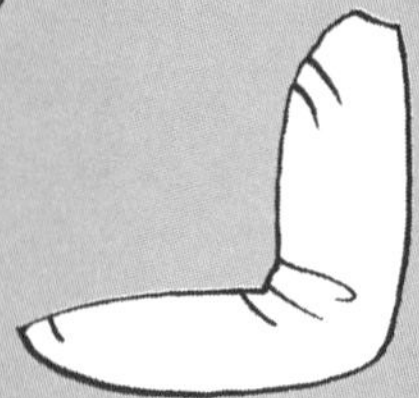
sock

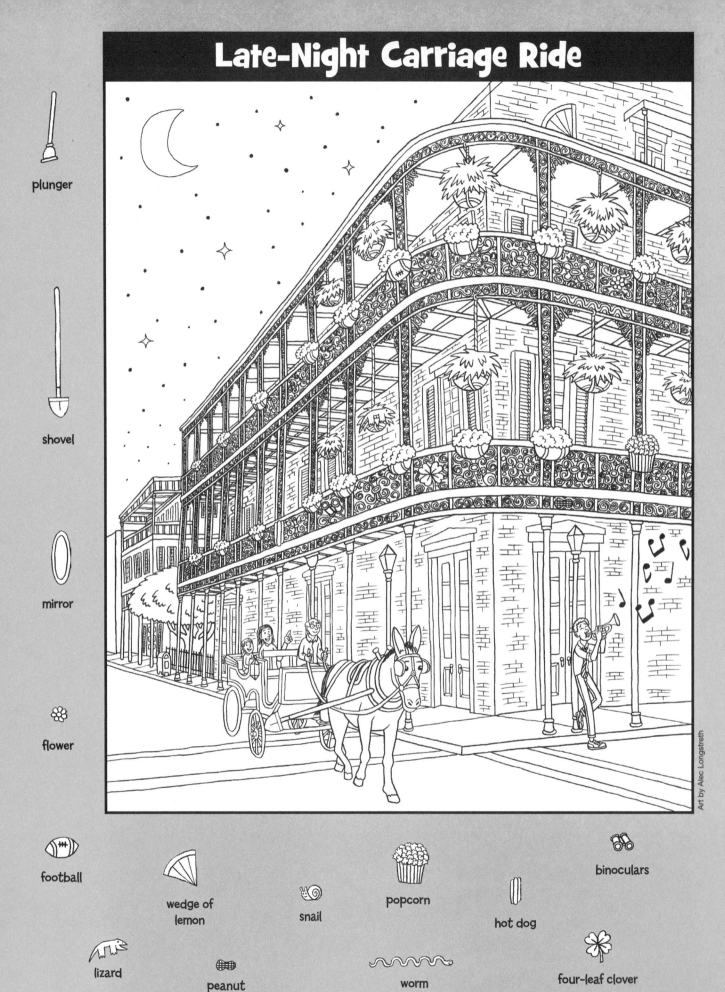

Late-Night Carriage Ride

plunger

shovel

mirror

flower

Art by Alec Longstreth

football

wedge of lemon

snail

popcorn

hot dog

binoculars

lizard

peanut

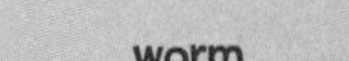
worm

four-leaf clover

Petting the Horses

Art by Susan Miller

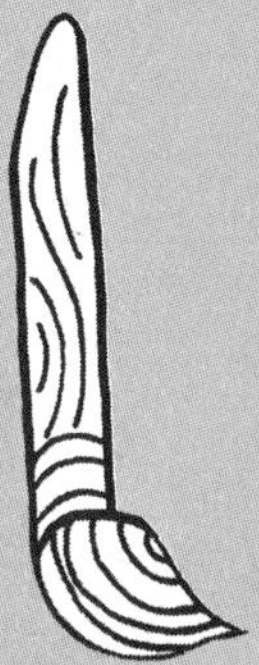

artist's brush

basketball

ice-cream cone

boot

toothbrush

banana

doughnut

mitten

Saddle Up

Art by Meryl Henderson

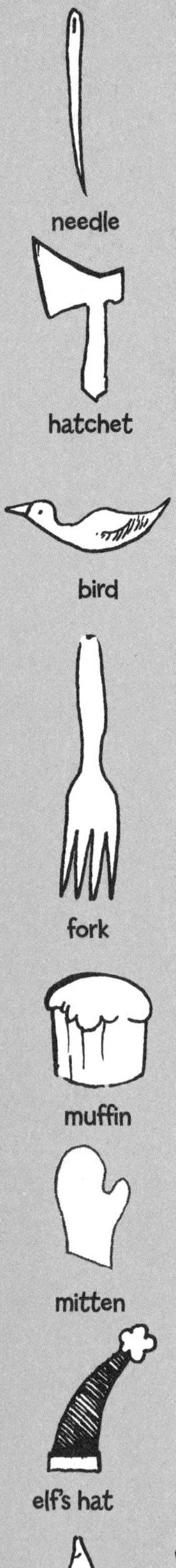

needle
hatchet
bird
fork
muffin
mitten
elf's hat
pencil

glove
2 bells
banana
crescent moon
heart
fish
fried egg
feather
bowl
dog bone
flag

Trot through Town

Art by Dave Clegg

flag
hoe
ladder
cane
artist's brush
chef's hat
sock
butterfly
slice of pizza
chili pepper
banana
saucepan
envelope
caterpillar
crescent moon
ruler
kite
boomerang
piece of popcorn
fish
lollipop

What a Sight!

golf club

drumstick

butter knife

ruler

mushroom

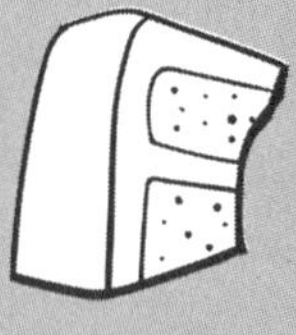

slice of cake

crown

candy kiss

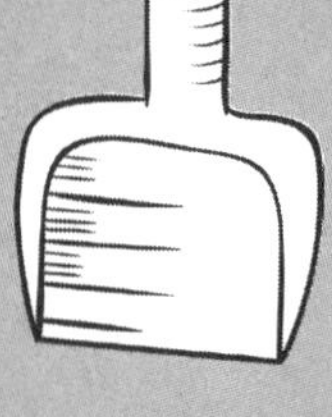

dustpan

boomerang

crescent moon

Art by Bill Golliher

artist's brush

nail

flag

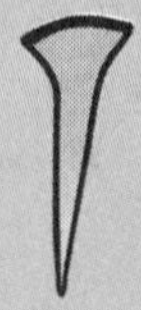

golf tee

slice of pizza

cookie

piece of popcorn

envelope

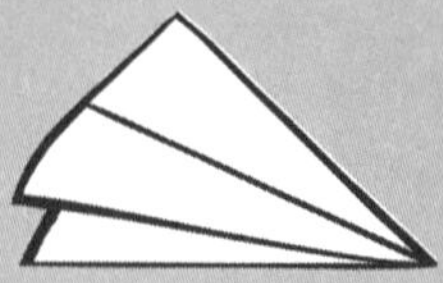

paper airplane

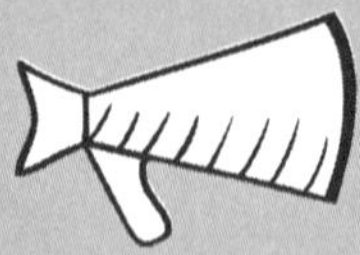

megaphone

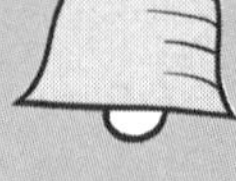

bell

Animal Derby

hockey stick
artist's brush
needle and thread
plunger
hammer
light bulb
paper clip
egg
tack
pointy hat
microphone
snake
wristwatch
domino
sock
jellyfish
game piece
iron
heart
Art by Arieh Zeldich

Parade Pride
needle
shovel
pencil
magic wand
ruler
spool of thread
hairpin
slice of pie
ice-cream cone
piece of popcorn
teardrop
snake
seashell
sock
megaphone
crown
crescent moon
Art by Apryl Stott

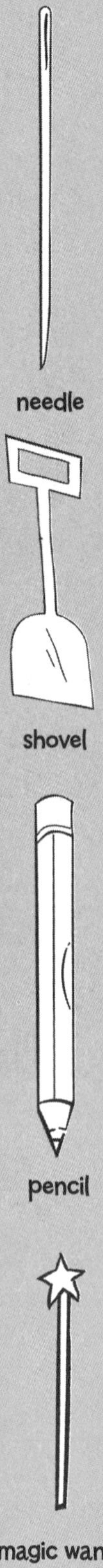

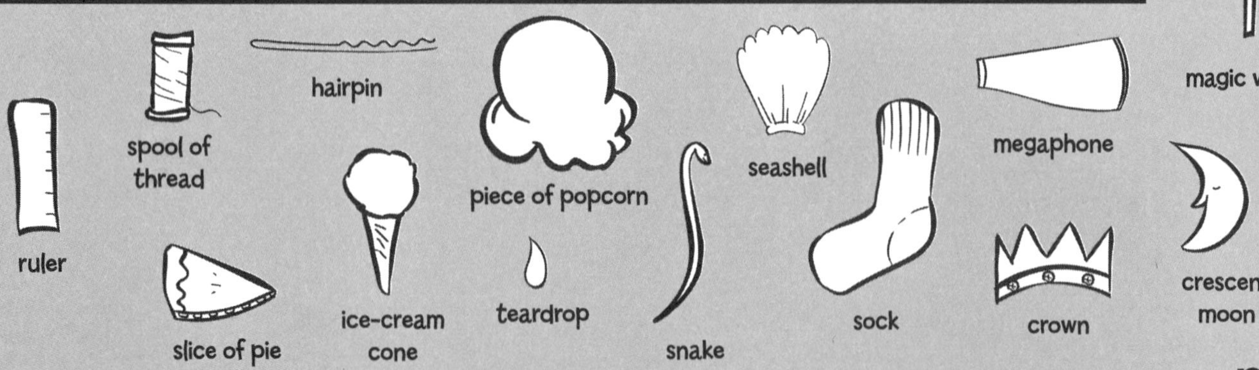

Barnyard Bingo

Art by Bill Golliher

feather

hockey stick

crescent moon

fishhook

flag

coat hanger

sock

paintbrush

mushroom

envelope

needle

strawberry

ruler

paper clip

butter knife

heart

ladle

mitten

light bulb

A Little Hoarse

Art by Jamie Smith

ax

comb

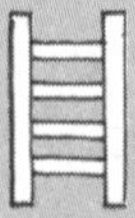

ladder

slice of pizza

pennant

banana

teacup

heart

crown

ice-cream bar

bow tie

golf ball

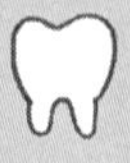

tooth

A Horse Shoo-In

paintbrush

toothbrush

golf club

bell

book

pennant

Art by Mike DeSantis

drinking straw

fork

ruler

heart

ice-cream cone

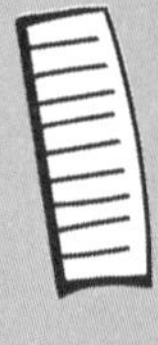

comb

The Hoof Patrol

Art by Ellen Appleby

flashlight

artist's brush

pen

bowling pin

needle

spoon

safety pin

paper clip

doughnut

ice-cream bar

pear

slice of bread

banana

frog

teacup

fork

heart

lock

lollipop

Winter Wanderers

Art by Dave Klug

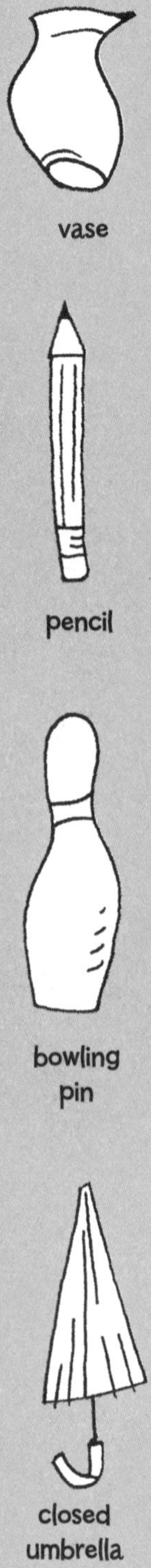

Horseshoe Shopping

Art by Tamara Petrosino

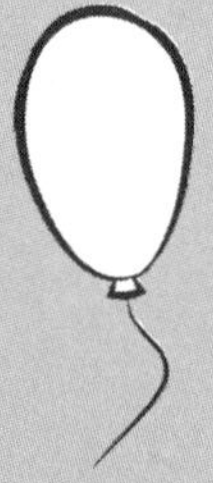
balloon

sailboat

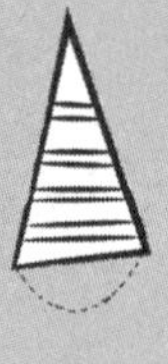
party hat

bowling pin

slice of pizza

envelope

leaf

crown

ruler

mushroom

flower

banana

Riding Class

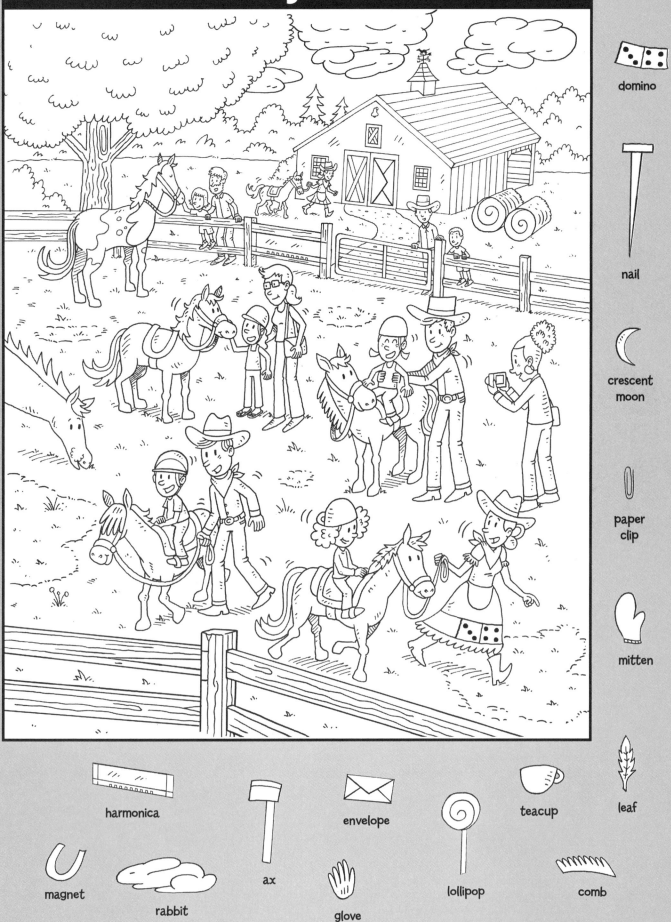

Art by Neil Numberman

domino

nail

crescent moon

paper clip

mitten

leaf

harmonica

envelope

teacup

magnet

rabbit

ax

glove

lollipop

comb

Pen Pals

Art by Paula Tabor

pencil

baseball bat

needle

artist's brush

heart

feather

pine tree

seashell

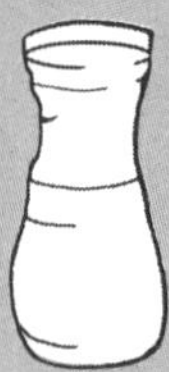

vase

fish

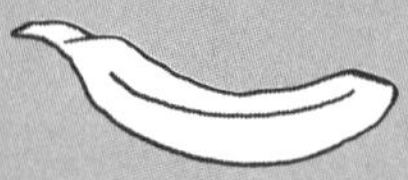

banana

bell

comb

spoon

Barrel Run
nail
pencil
toothbrush
closed umbrella
cane
cotton candy
book
bowl
wishbone
pennant
banana
arrow
heart
flag
carrot
Art by Sally Springer

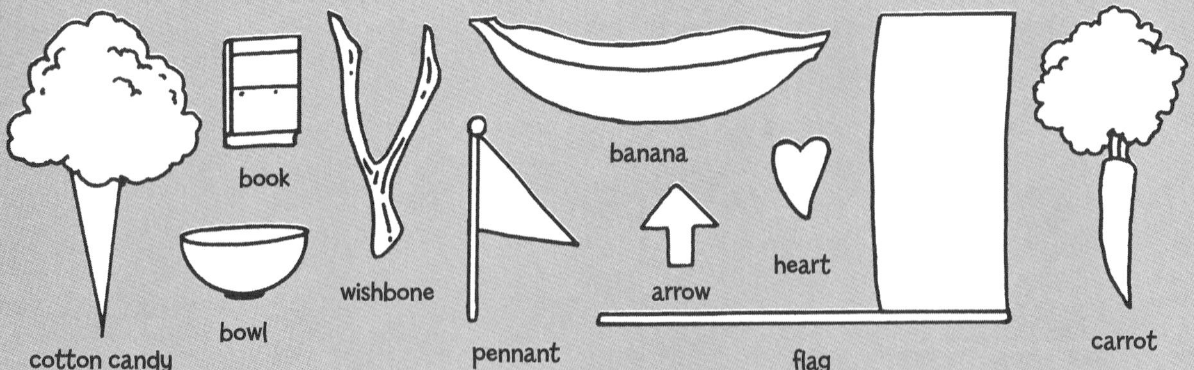

A *Baa*-d Witness

Art by Ron Lieser

artist's brush

oar

candle

flag

drinking straw

banana

screw

crescent moon

caterpillar

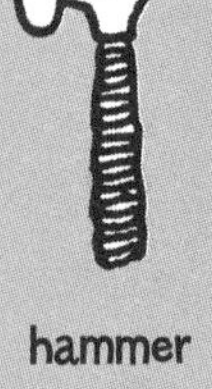

hammer

funnel

bowl

lollipop

fishhook

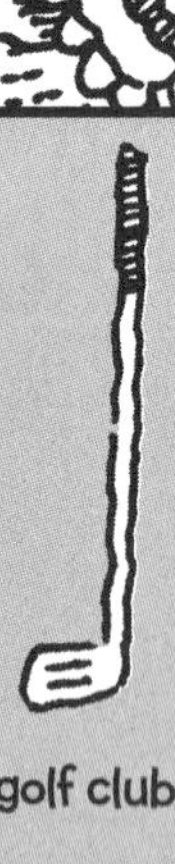

golf club

A Brisk Trot

Art by Chuck Dillon

fishhook

wishbone

candle

banana

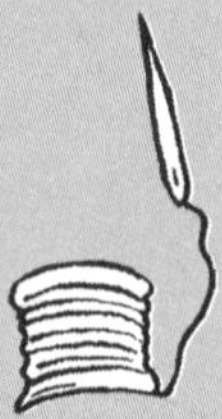
needle and thread

penguin

bell

teacup

flashlight

trowel

spoon

mouse

knitted hat

bowling pin

shark

boomerang

carrot

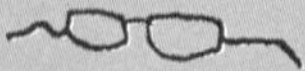
eyeglasses

All the Queen's Horses

Art by Arieh Zeldich

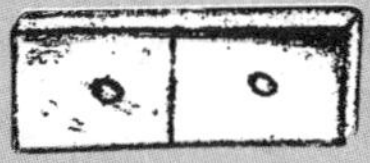

domino

fishhook

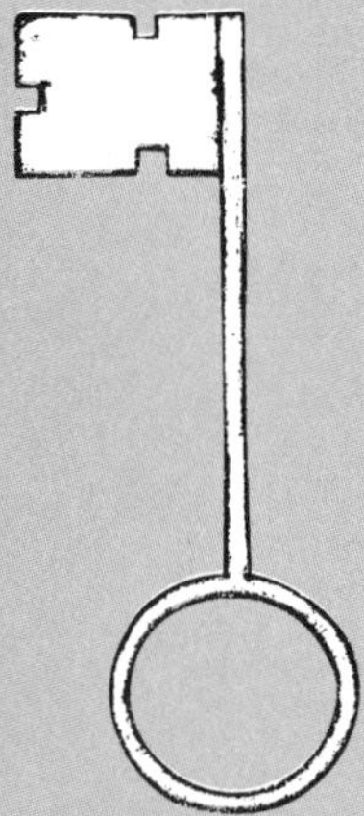

key

ice-cream bar

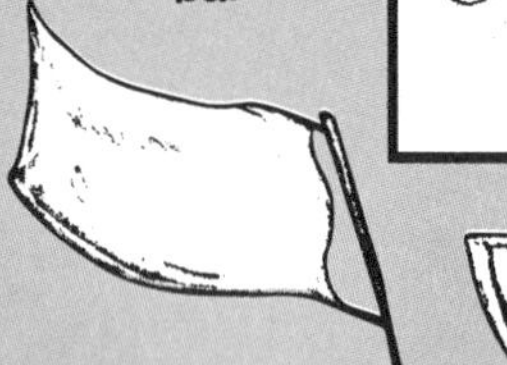

flag

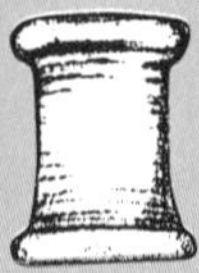

spool of thread

wedge of lemon

crown

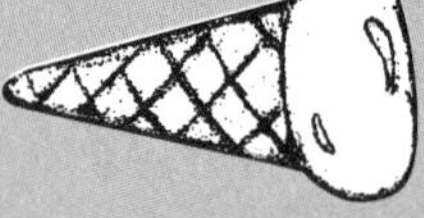

ice-cream cone

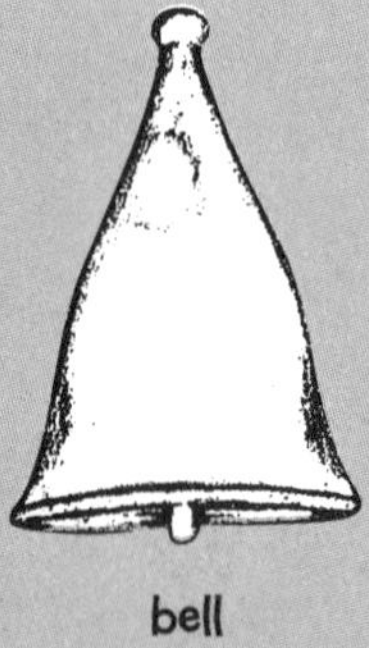

bell

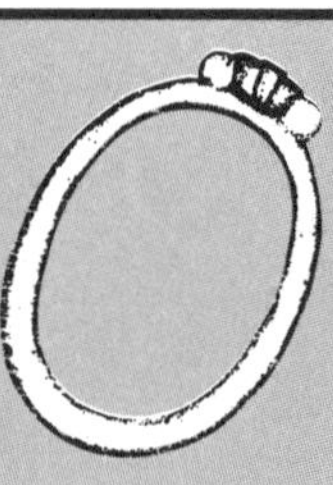

ring

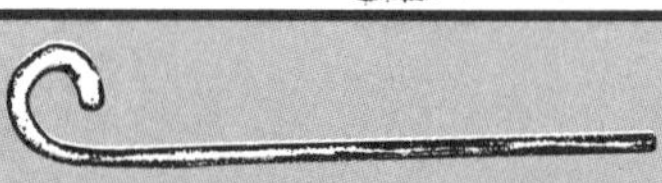

cane

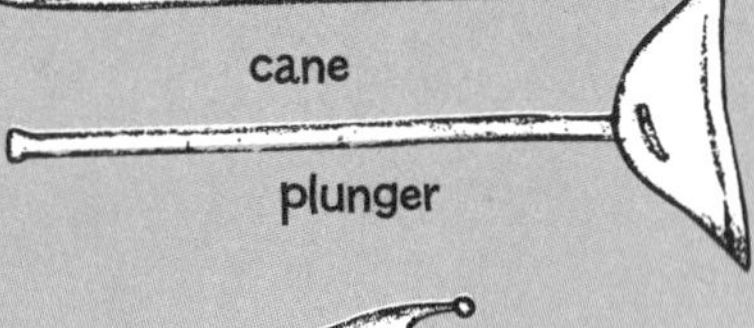

plunger

closed umbrella

On the Fence
nail
needle
comb
fishhook
wishbone
pennant
flag
sailboat
banana
musical note
heart
slice of cake
wristwatch
closed umbrella
bowl
Art by Sally Springer

Visiting the Farm

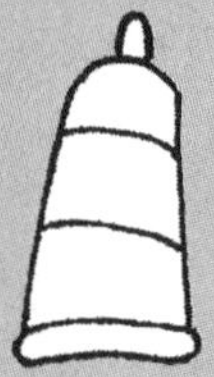
tube of toothpaste

feather

glove

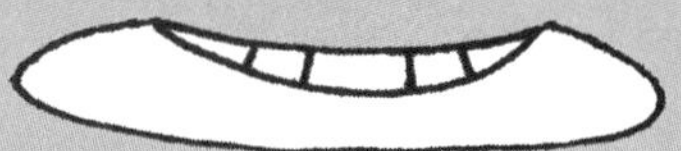
canoe

toothbrush

comb

Art by Ron Lieser

wristwatch

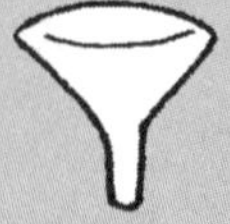

funnel

teacup

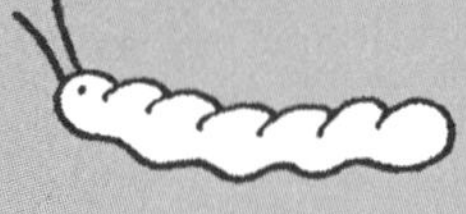

caterpillar

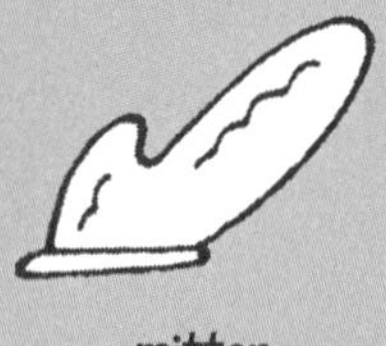

mitten

heart

Barnyard Bonding

Art by Maggie Swanson

toothbrush

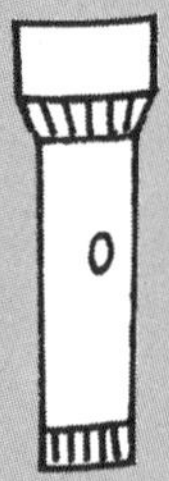

flashlight

sock

ice-cream cone

pineapple

muffin

teacup

glove

2 birds

slice of cake

mitten

lemon

Show Jumping
needle
heart
lollipop
paintbrush
candle
dolphin
carrot
mushroom
funnel
horn
ring
screwdriver
pennant
bell
tack
sailboat
hat
slice of pie
toothbrush
crescent moon
Art by Linda Weller

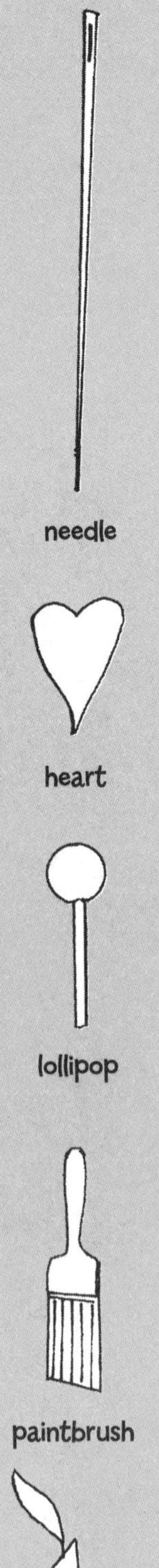

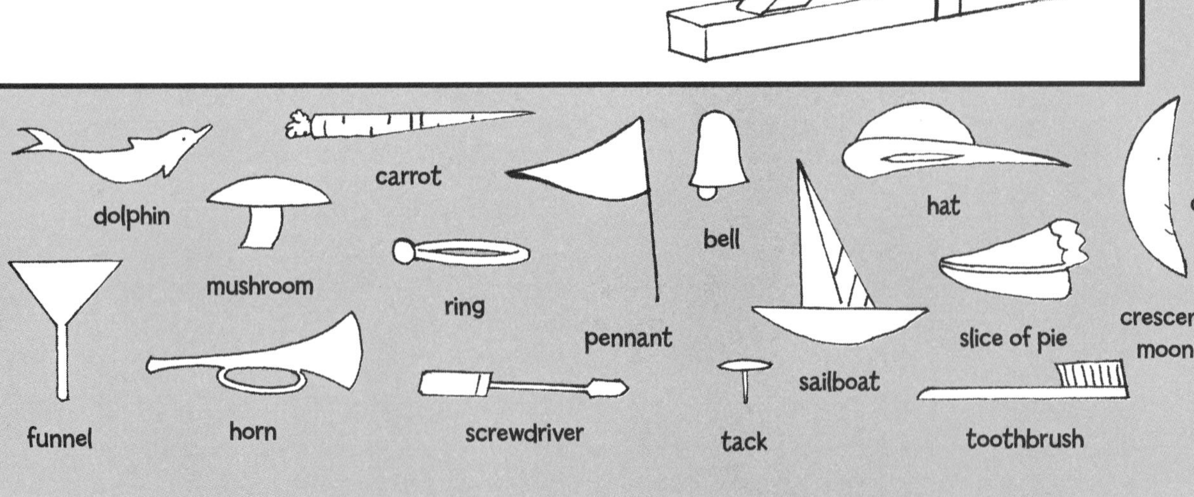

Food and Friends

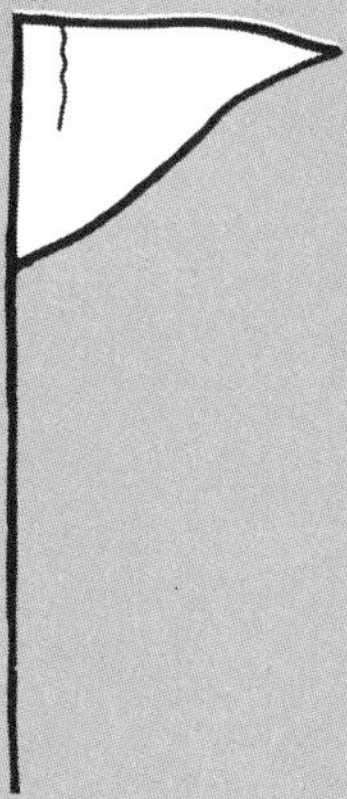

pennant

pair of pants

artist's brush

fishhook

Art by Katy Davis

closed umbrella

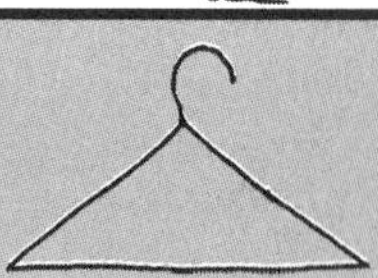

coat hanger

dolphin

rabbit

teacup

pear

mitten

football

Found on the Farm

Art by Tim Davis

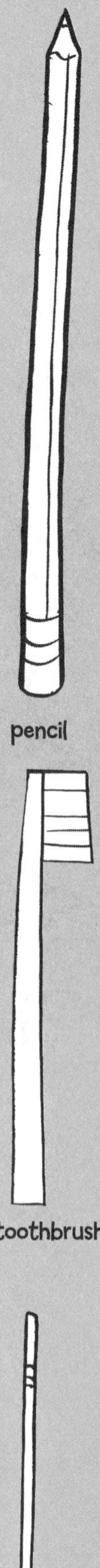

Horse Spotting

Art by George Wildman

artist's brush

carrot

baby's bottle

lamp

pennant

slice of pizza

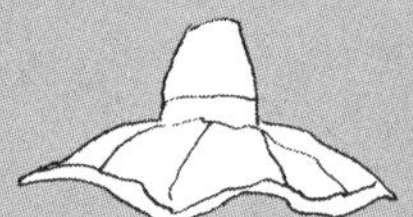

hat

pear

heart

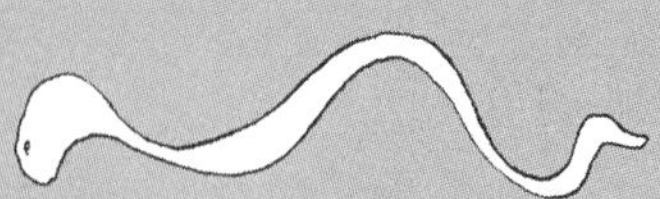

snake

crescent moon

baseball cap

bird

open book

Firefighter Fillies

Art by George Wildman

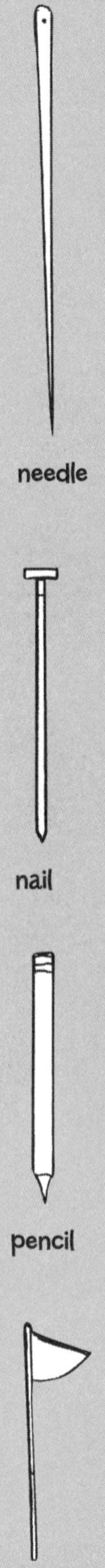

Trailblazers
paintbrush
lollipop
needle
toothbrush
pennant
heart
carrot
screwdriver
mushroom
hat
funnel
tack
candle
bell
sailboat
horn
dolphin
mug
crescent moon
ring
slice of pie
Art by Linda Weller

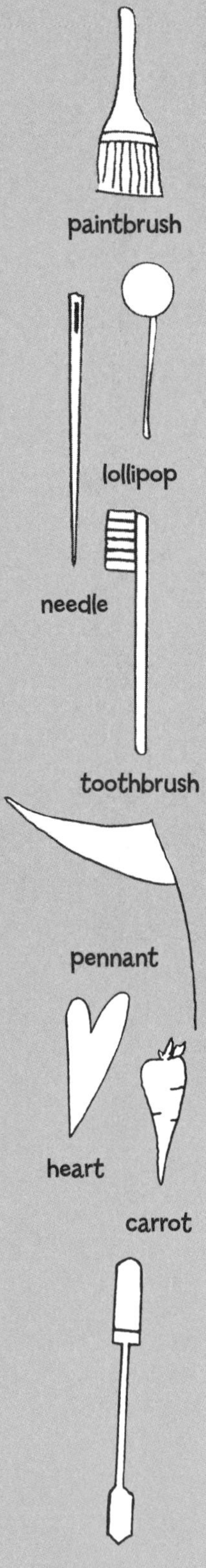

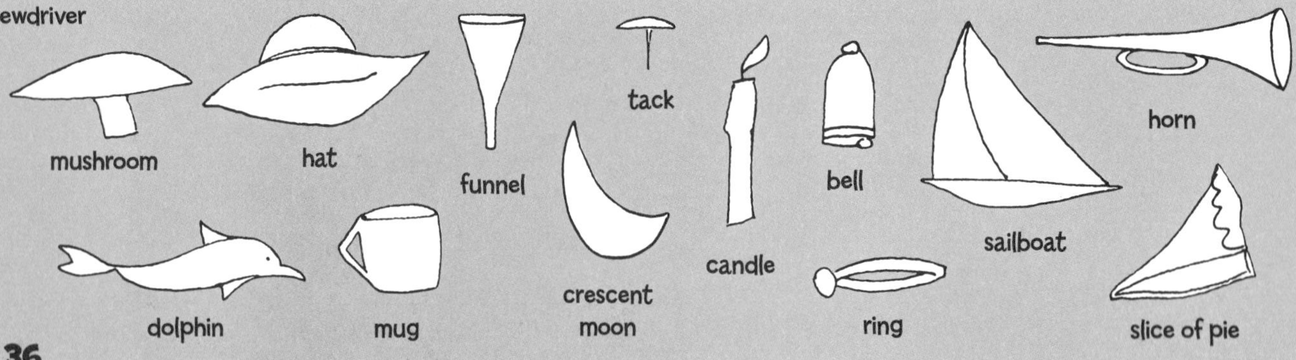

Feeding Time
artist's brush
ice-cream cone
tack
hammer
paintbrush
shoe
toothbrush
saw
mouse
tube of toothpaste
bird
pie
ladle
worm
Art by Holly Rand

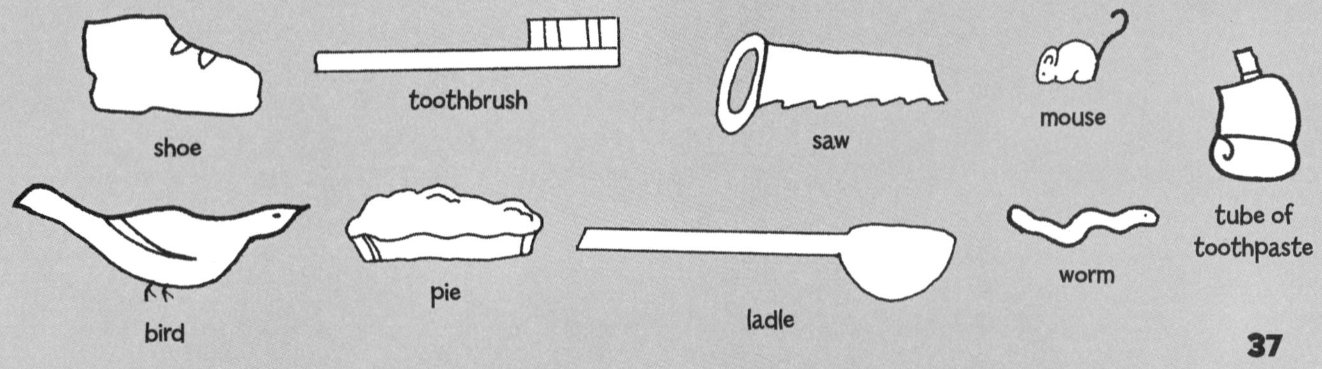

Horsepower

artist's brush

cotton candy

needle

golf club

nail

ring

bell

mug

clothespin

baseball cap

egg

mushroom

Art by George Wildman

caterpillar

slice of lemon

funnel

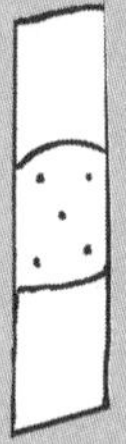
adhesive bandage

baseball bat

lollipop

olive

magnet

book

bird

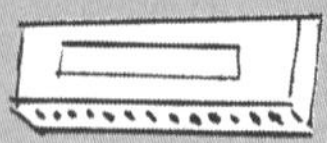
harmonica

slice of pizza

Merry-Go-Round
pennant
golf club
screw
nail
Art by Sally Springer
fishing rod
snake
arrow
teacup
pear
slice of pie
horseshoe
mug
musical note
zipper
crescent moon
needle
fishhook
question mark
ring

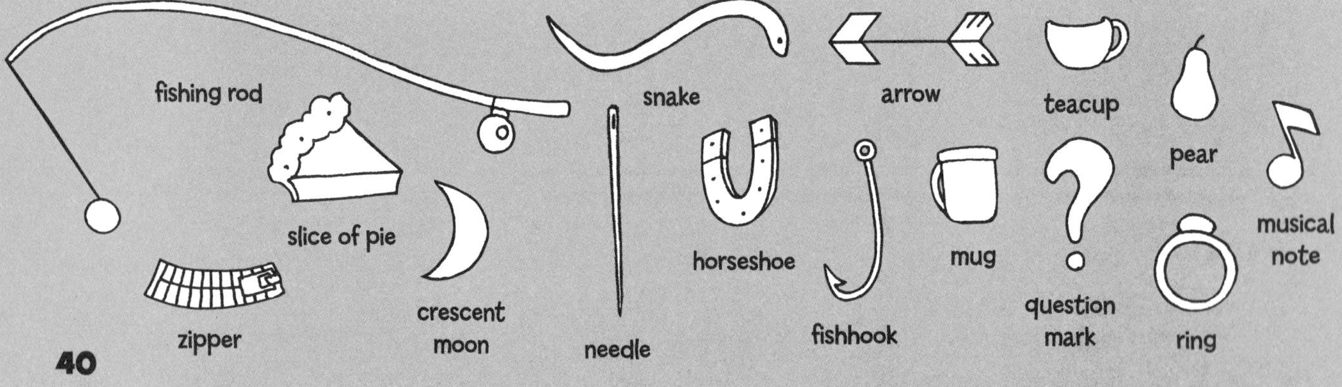

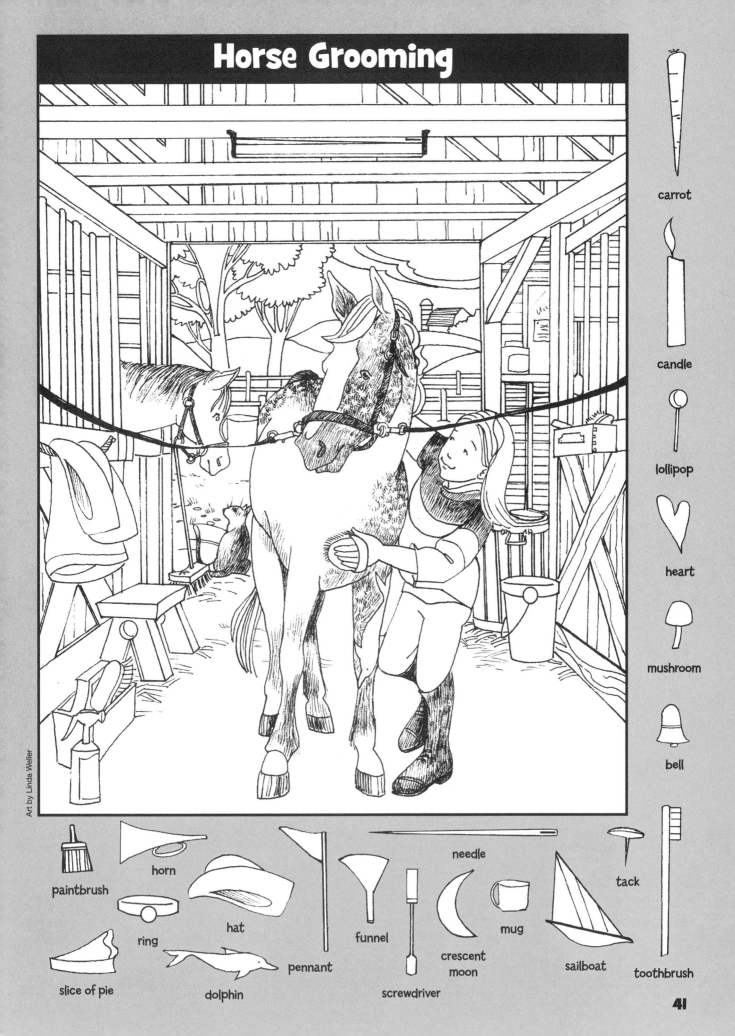

Horse Grooming

Art by Linda Weller

carrot
candle
lollipop
heart
mushroom
bell
paintbrush
horn
ring
hat
slice of pie
dolphin
pennant
needle
funnel
screwdriver
crescent moon
mug
tack
sailboat
toothbrush

Country Music

Art by R. Michael Palan

carrot

candle

toothbrush

sock

needle

spool of thread

slipper

tube of toothpaste

ring

fish

fishhook

spoon

hammer

acorn

Leaping through Life

Art by Tim Davis

artist's brush

butterfly

bird

hammer

paper clip

star

fish

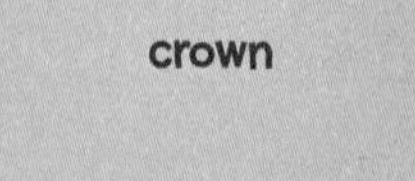

crown

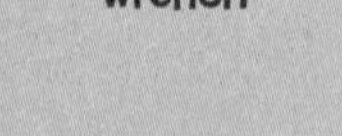

wrench

duck

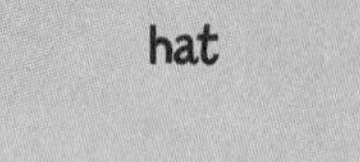

hat

mouse

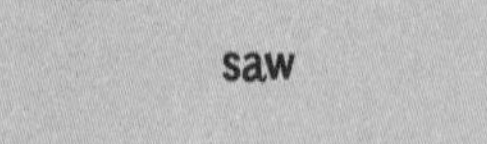

saw

Hayride

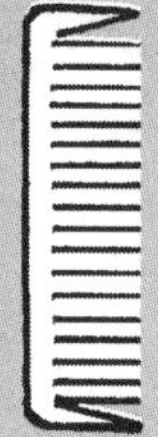
comb

glove

toothbrush

crescent moon

fish

leaf

Art by Ron Lieser

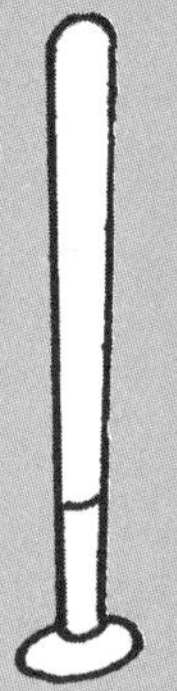

baseball bat

carrot

ring

banana

wristwatch

slice of pie

Post Time
crescent moon
screwdriver
candle
bell
pennant
hat
needle
dolphin
slice of pie
mug
horn
mushroom
toothbrush
paintbrush
sailboat
carrot
tack
ring
funnel
heart
lollipop
Art by Linda Weller

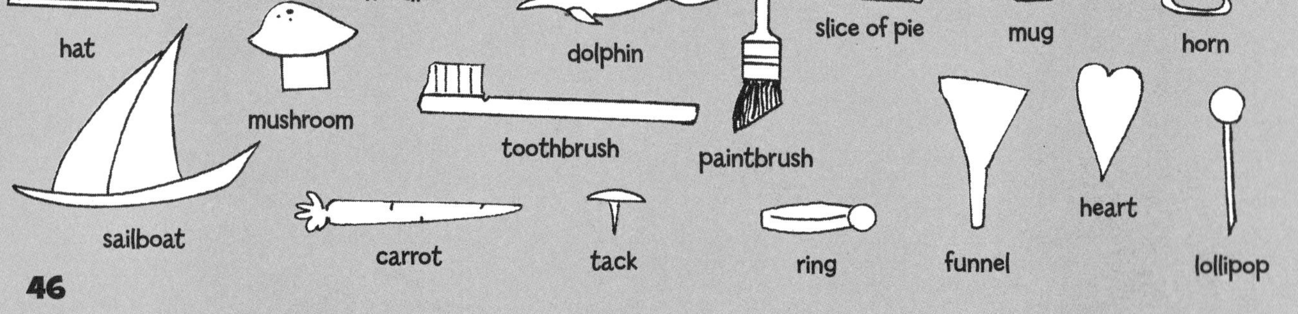

Yeehaw!

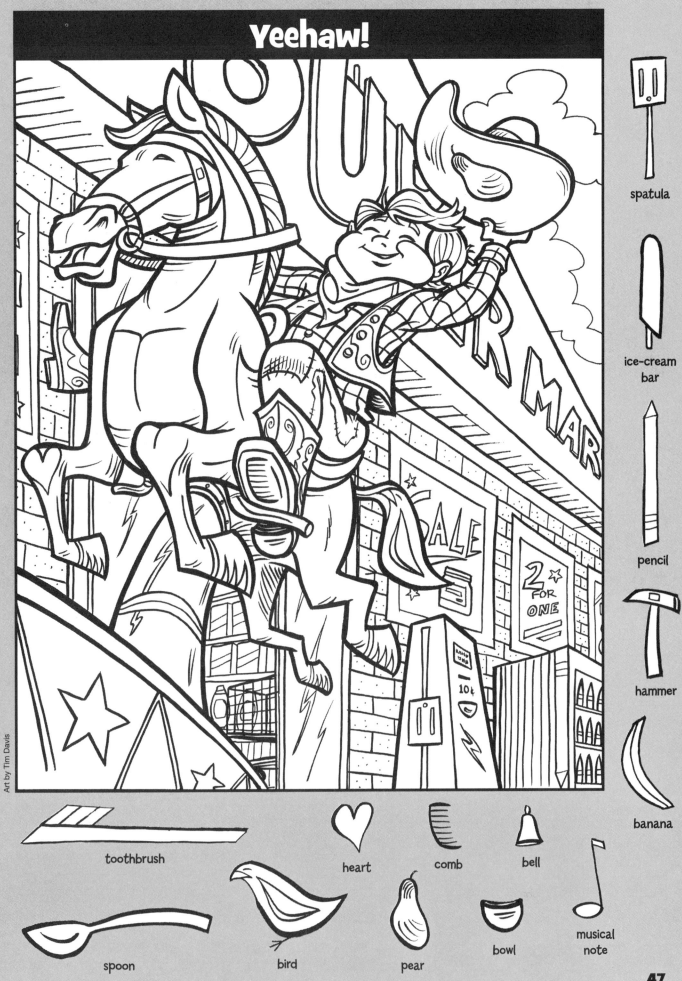

Art by Tim Davis

spatula

ice-cream bar

pencil

hammer

banana

toothbrush

heart

comb

bell

musical note

spoon

bird

pear

bowl

Horse Limbo

Art by Jef Czkaj

scissors

slice of pizza

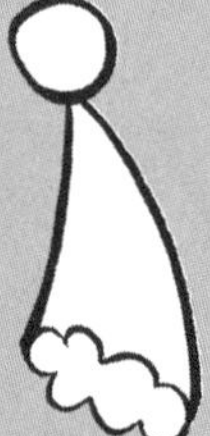
elf's hat

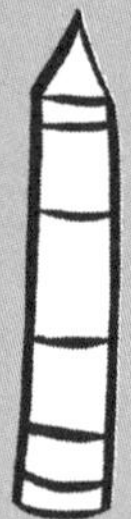
crayon

fish

ghost

banana

crown

tack

hatchet

teacup

Wagon Party

Art by Kit Wray

pencil

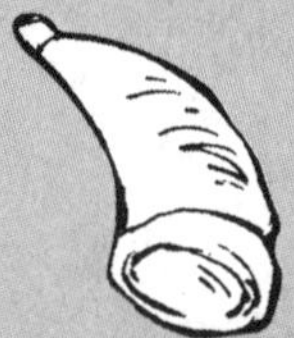

elf's hat

crescent moon

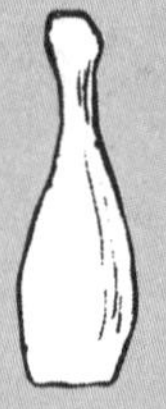

bowling pin

teacup

briefcase

bird

chicken

mallet

feather

mushroom

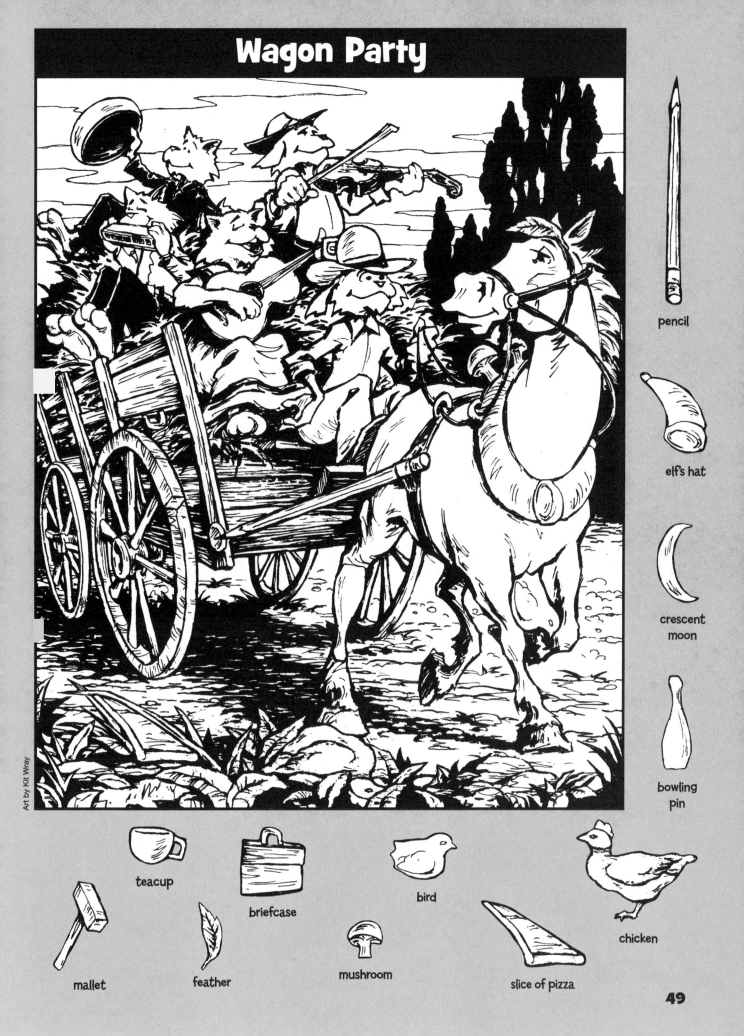

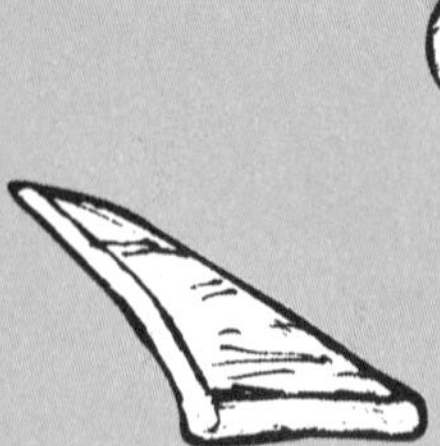

slice of pizza

Pasture Pals
candle
banana
mallet
ladle
shark
bird
chick
open book
mushroom
dog
seal
hat
duck
boot
Art by Leslie Franz

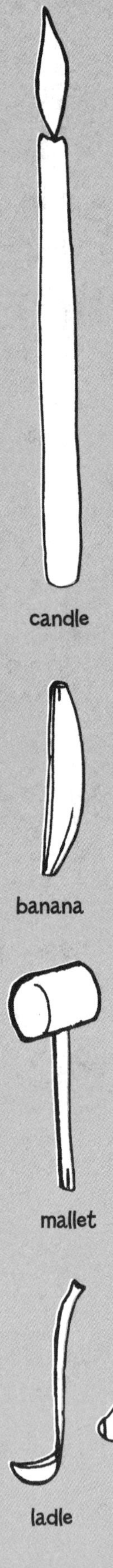

Neigh-ture
Art by Carolyn Conahan
fishing pole
banana
hairbrush
frying pan
bird
shovel
pennant
mouse
rabbit
squirrel
saltshaker
needle
bowl

Carousel Corral

peppermint stick

screw

crescent moon

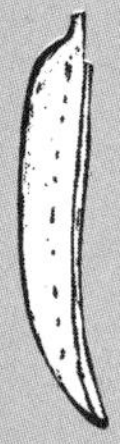

banana

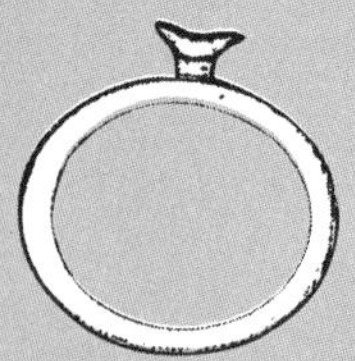

ring

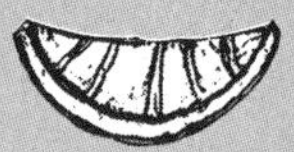

wedge of lemon

muffin

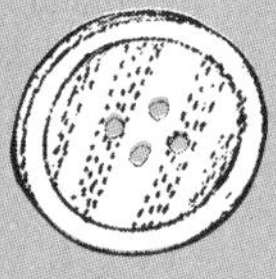

button

apple

ice-cream cone

book

bowl

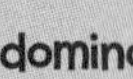

domino

Art by Arieh Zeldich

stick of candy

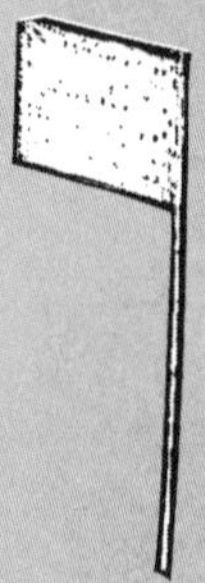

flag

pear

coffeepot

paper clip

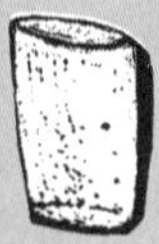

drinking glass

light bulb

heart

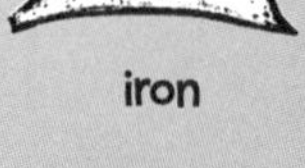

iron

spool of thread

cherry

egg

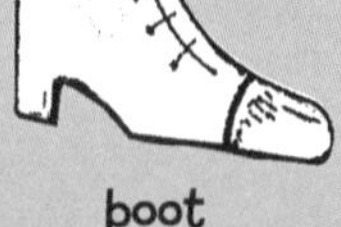

boot

Sleigh Ride

Art by Jennifer Harney

- toothbrush
- sock
- hockey stick
- ladder
- leaf
- spool of thread
- candy cane
- dog bone
- paper clip
- traffic cone
- bell
- book
- lollipop
- party hat
- pencil
- doughnut
- banana
- lightning bolt
- snail
- ruler
- heart
- diamond
- worm
- slice of pizza
- wedge of lemon
- teacup
- arrow

Done for the Day
carrot
candle
hockey stick
hammer
closed umbrella
fork
hatchet
potholder
lampshade
bug
canoe
sock
baseball bat
slice of bread
handbag
bird
worm
Art by Elizabeth Allyn

Stable Mates
artist's brush
clothespin
ladle
arrow
hammer
ice-cream cone
boot
sailboat
dinosaur
pig
cat
key
bird
paintbrush
Art by Leslie Franz

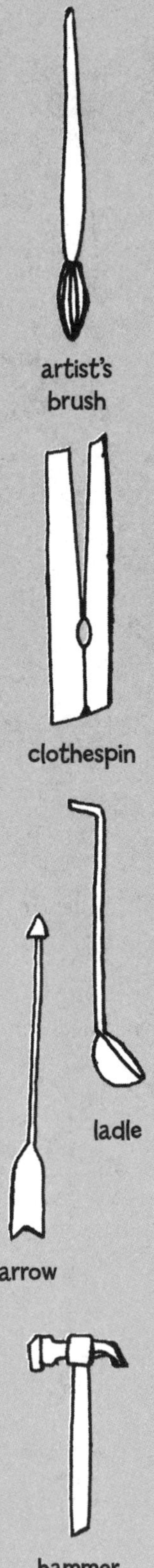

For the Win

banana

artist's brush

slice of pizza

feather

lollipop

ring

needle

broccoli

heart

book

rabbit

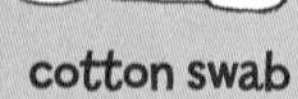
cotton swab

sailboat

pitcher

ice-cream cone

Art by Neil Numberman

Promenade

Art by Elizabeth Allyn

- ice-cream cone
- boot
- ruler
- hammer
- wrench
- ice skate
- book
- mouse
- flashlight
- banana
- pear
- needle
- iron
- spoon
- bird
- scrub brush
- slice of pie
- toothbrush

Follow the Leader

Art by Leslie Franz

candle

ice-cream bar

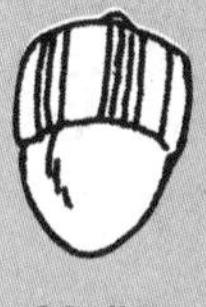

acorn

ring

mitten

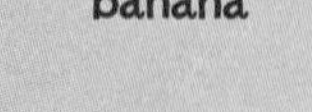

banana

snail

turtle

goose

bird

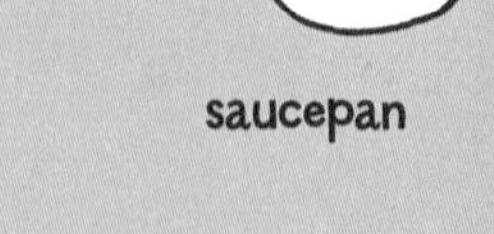

saucepan

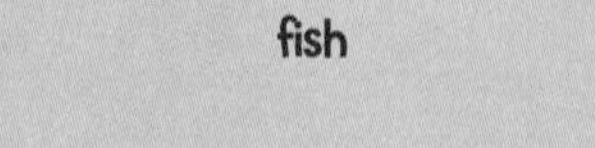

fish

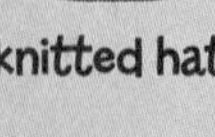

knitted hat

A Horse, of Course!

Art by Sally Springer

pencil

artist's brush

needle

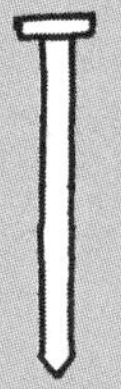

nail

jar

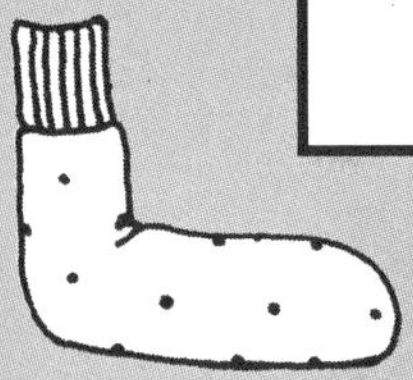

sock

rabbit

saw

wishbone

fishhook

toothbrush

heart

key

star

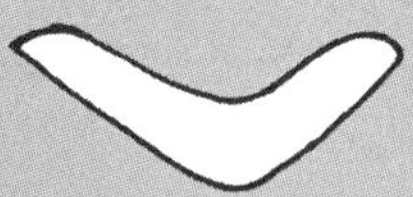

boomerang

sailboat

crown

mouse

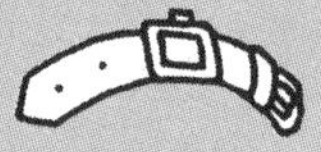

wristwatch

crescent moon

Back in the Saddle
spoon
shovel
heart
teardrop
ice-cream cone
banana
flag
glove
fish
needle
paper clip
high-heeled shoe
pencil
crescent moon
sailboat
slice of pie
Art by Tim Davis

Around and Around

Art by Shawn Berlute-Shea

mitten

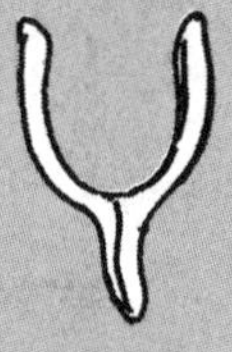

wishbone

candle

turnip

seal

fish

3 birds

yo-yo

ice-cream cone

roller skate

Learning to Ride

Art by Linda Weller

toothbrush

spoon

needle

candle

bird

cupcake

mug

ice-cream cone

book

flowerpot

carrot

saucepan

fish

shoe

scrub brush

tack

boot

flashlight

slice of pie

Whoa, Horsey!

party hat

baseball bat

pickle

banana

saucepan

slice of bread

candle

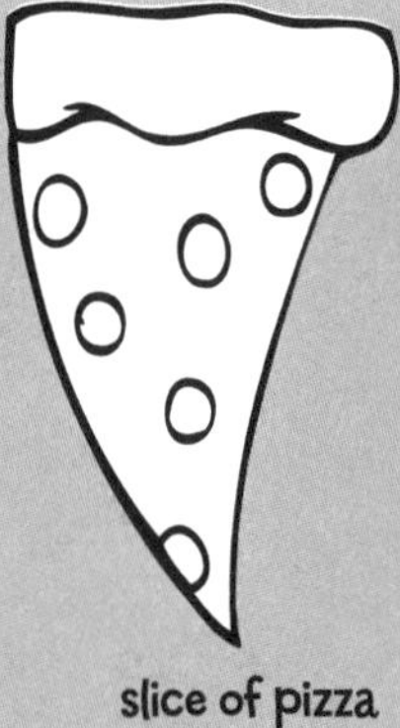
slice of pizza

mug

toothbrush

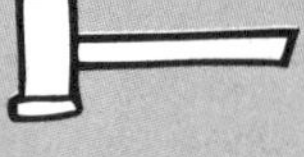
mallet

book

Art by Mary Sullivan

needle

carrot

fishhook

pennant

closed umbrella

wishbone

bowl

funnel

butterfly

bowling pin

heart

arrow

snake

Good Stable Manners

Art by Patrick Girouard

slice of pizza

banana

pen

paper clip

drinking straw

magnet

piece of popcorn

fish

envelope

eyeglasses

golf ball

bell

The Ranch

Art by Patrick Coleman

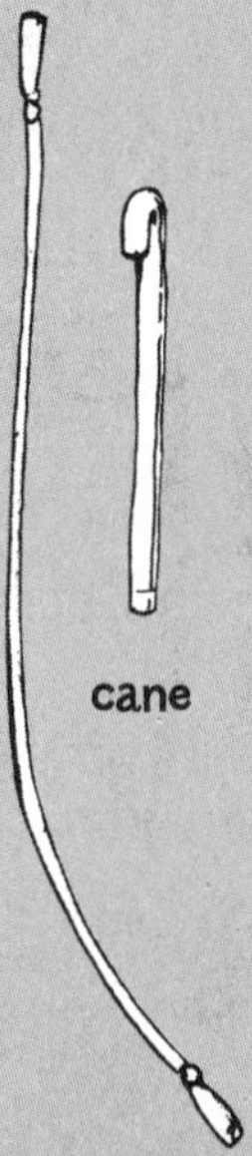

cane

jump rope

spoon

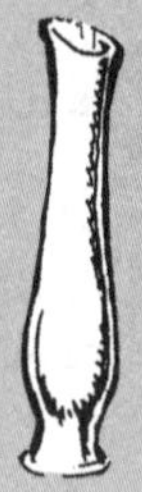

vase

hockey stick

book

fish

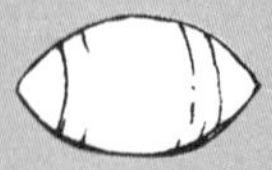

football

toothbrush

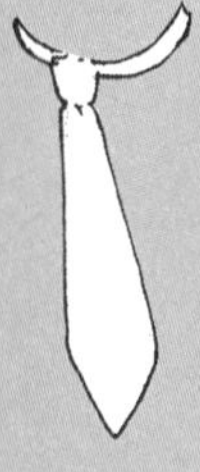

necktie

paper airplane

pencil

cupcake

Nightmare

Art by Tim Davis

toothbrush

artist's brush

banana

spoon

fish

bat

heart

bottle

bell

glove

sailboat

carrot

Horse Roller Derby

Art by Sonya Montenegro

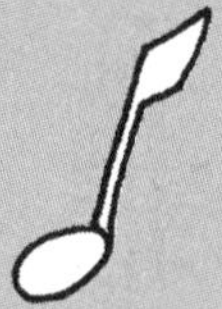
musical note

sock

mushroom

lightning bolt

feather

traffic cone

saucepan

magnet

top hat

boomerang

heart

canoe

sailboat

arrow

crown

Mane Street

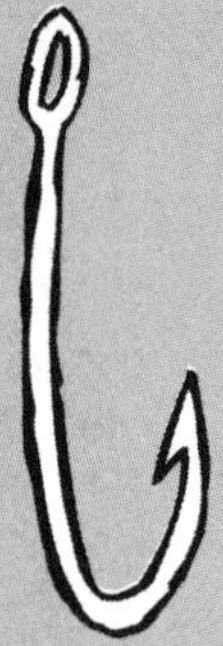

fishhook

envelope

ruler

mitten

snake

canoe

boot

Art by Rich Powell

kite

pennant

tube of toothpaste

pie

fish

flashlight

teacup

slice of pizza

Racing Tracks

Art by R. Michael Palan

broom

flashlight

crayon

shovel

hammer

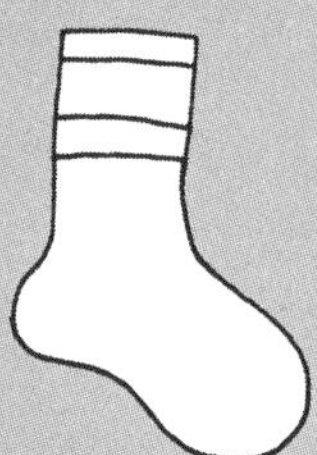

sock

slice of pizza

spoon

crescent moon

fish

nail

wristwatch

Open Road

Art by Elizabeth Allyn

cat

carrot

feather

turkey

loaf of bread

pitcher

mitten

mouse

fish

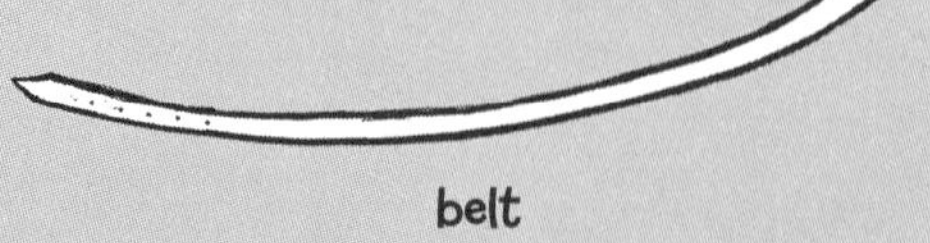

belt

ice skate

book

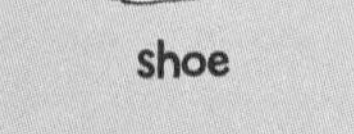

shoe

Trails and Tails

artist's brush

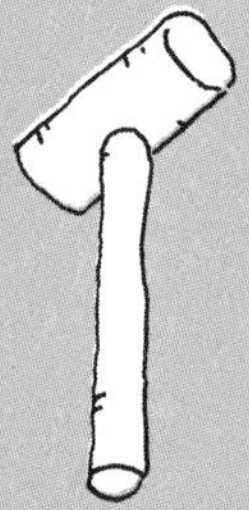

mallet

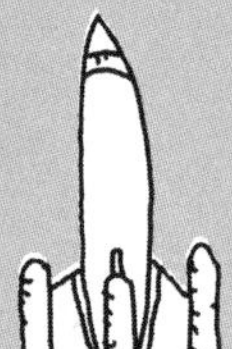

rocket ship

Art by Charles Jordan

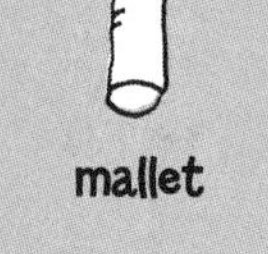

book

ladle

cupcake

crayon

pencil

oilcan

safety pin

bell

key

A New Friend

Art by Patrick Coleman

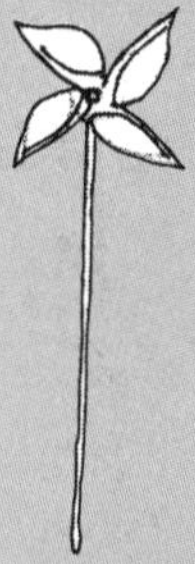

pinwheel

paintbrush

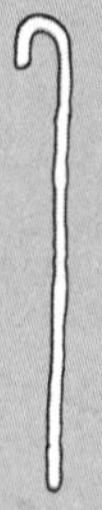

cane

pencil

pliers

mug

toothbrush

comb

slice of bread

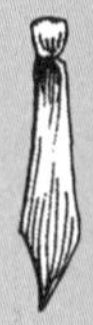

necktie

envelope

spool of thread

open book

Gaited Community

artist's brush

toothbrush

ax

flag

snake

open book

tack

Art by R. Michael Palan

spoon

fishhook

comb

ring

feather

wristwatch

hat

Cowboys and Cacti

Art by R. Michael Palan

pencil

tack

ring

carrot

crescent moon

teddy bear

teacup

hammer

kettle

screw

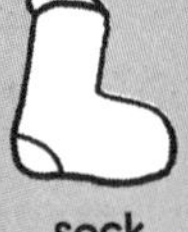

sock

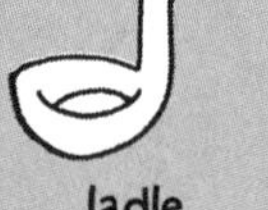

ladle

paintbrush

mitten

slice of pie

Don't Stirrup Too Much Trouble!

Art by R. Michael Palan

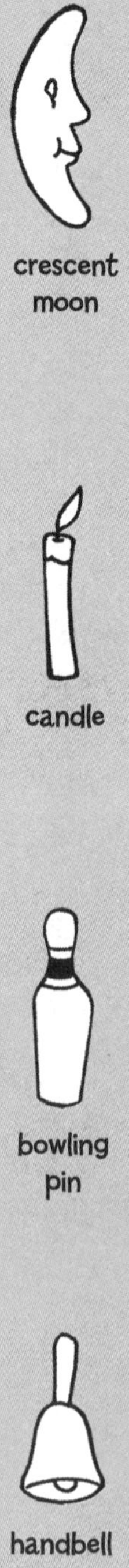

Ready to Ride

ruler

banana

tennis racket

rocket ship

Art by Kelly Kennedy

rowboat

raindrop

ring

radish

rose

Barnyard Buddies

Art by Dave Klug

glove

crown

banana

button

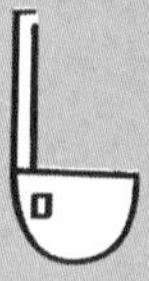

ladle

heart

comb

ring

boot

crescent moon

Pony Party

lollipop

ice-cream cone

crescent moon

olive

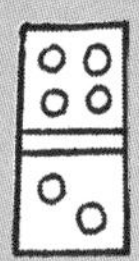
domino

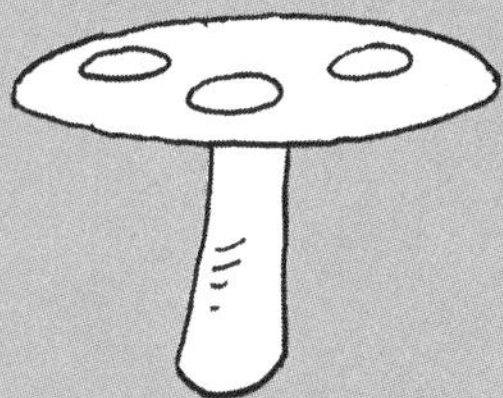
mushroom

rabbit

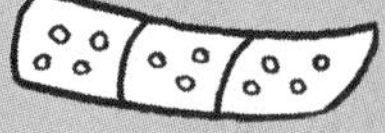
adhesive bandage

broccoli

comb

Art by Neil Numberman

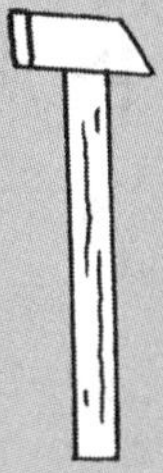

hammer

asparagus

fishhook

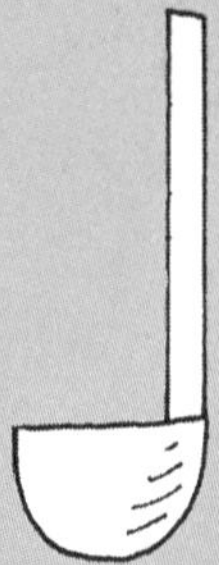

ladle

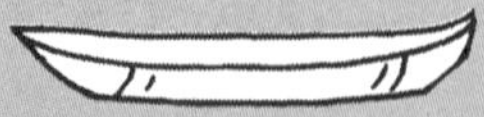

canoe

glove

snail

ghost

envelope

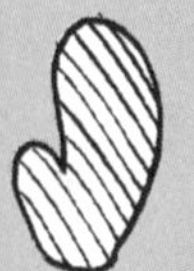

mitten

At the Amusement Park

Art by P. Melillo

golf club

anchor

owl

boot

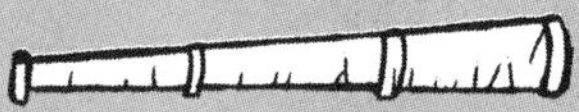

telescope

horseshoe

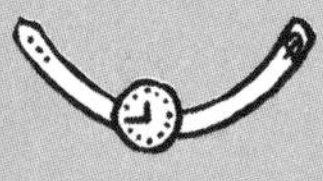

wristwatch

acorn

fish

bird

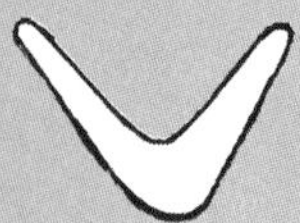

boomerang

umbrella

bell

New Shoes

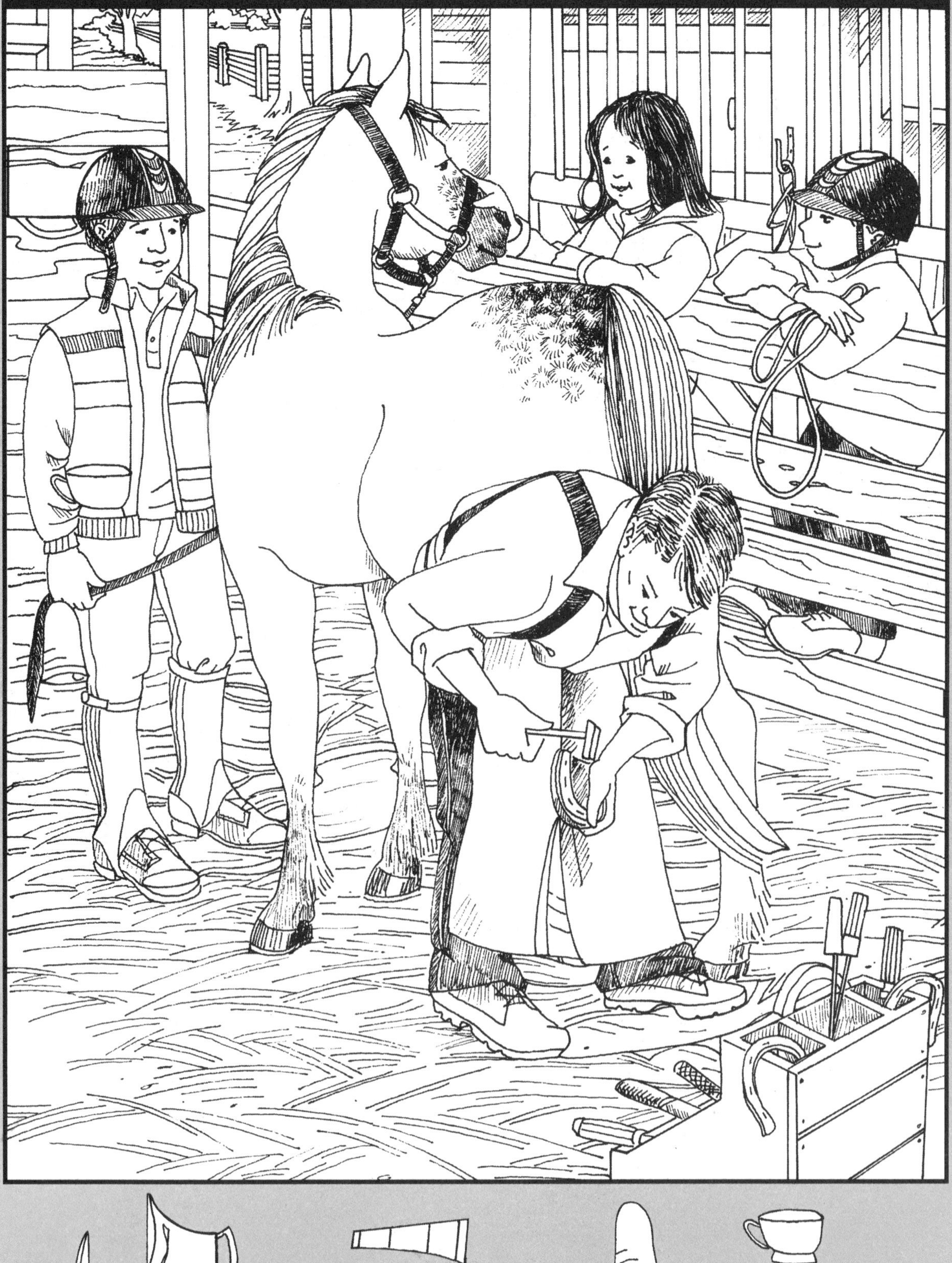

Art by Linda Weller

- candle
- mallet
- flashlight
- crayon
- sailboat
- pitcher
- telescope
- slice of bread
- mushroom
- sock
- bell
- teacup
- canoe
- fish
- spoon

Circling the Corral

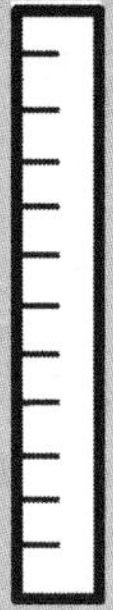
ruler

screwdriver

pine tree

saw

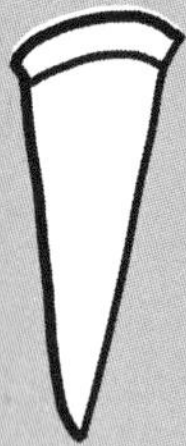
slice of pie

hot dog

crayon

light bulb

stamp

iron

envelope

egg

feather

Art by Dana Regan

golf club
hammer
artist's brush
candle
potato
leaf
wedge of lemon
ice pop
bell
adhesive bandage
kite

Rocking Horse

Art by Hector Borlasca

arrow

pencil

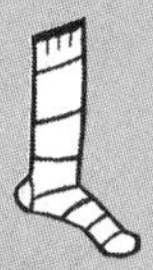
sock

screw

slice of pizza

ruler

football

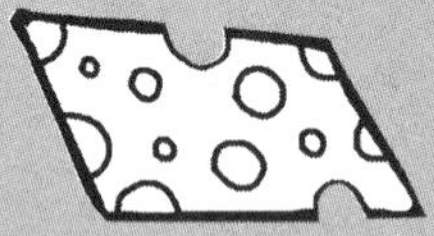
slice of cheese

baseball

high-heeled shoe

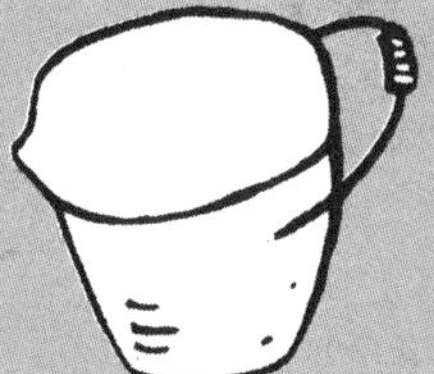
bucket

fork

Giddyup!

Art by Kate Salley Palmer

alligator

snake

cane

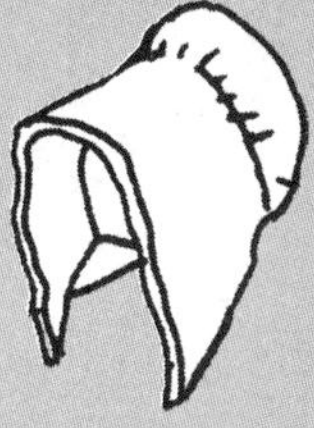

bonnet

spatula

cat

canoe

mouse

bowl

chicken

sneaker

teacup

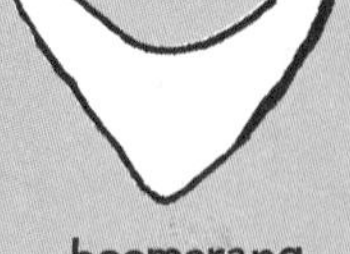

boomerang

Duck, Duck, Horse

Art by Mij Colson-Barnum

lantern

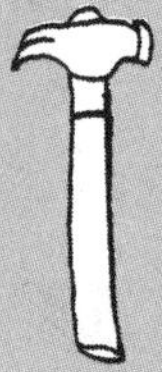

hammer

carrot

toothbrush

juicer

bell

bear

swan

lamb

pie

hat

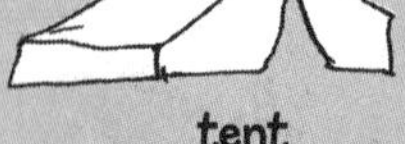

tent

lizard

star

Corral Group

Art by Mary Sullivan

sock

candle

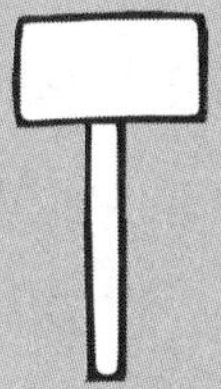

mallet

traffic cone

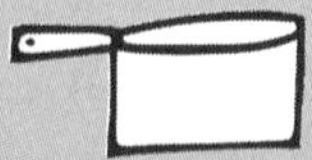

saucepan

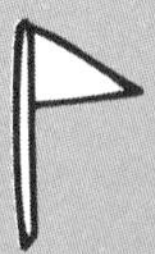

pennant

magnet

book

mushroom

birdhouse

flowerpot

shoe

Harvest Time

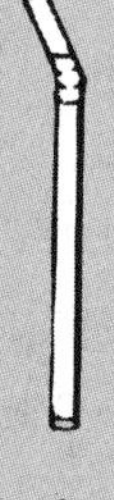

drinking straw

broom

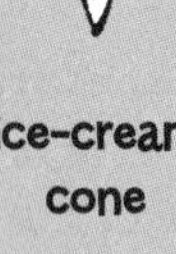

ice-cream cone

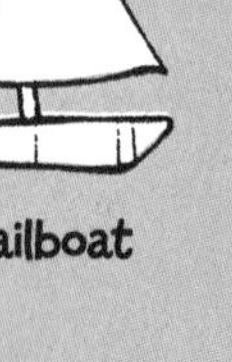

sailboat

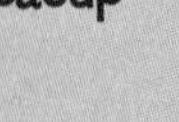

teacup

spoon

Art by Ellen Appleby

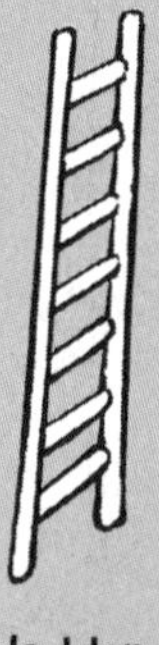

ladder

pencil

crescent moon

open book

glove

envelope

After the Fair

Art by Charles Jordan

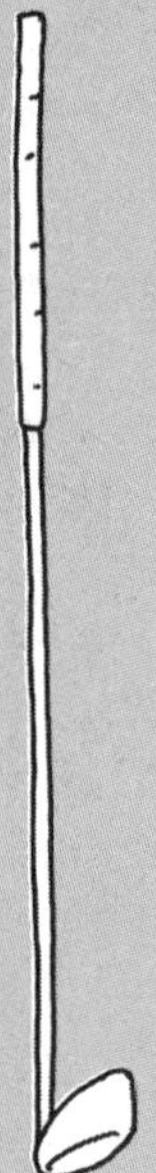

golf club

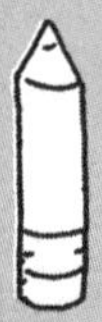

pencil

key

toothbrush

mitten

slice of cake

crown

tube of toothpaste

spoon

book

teacup

slice of pie

River Trail

Art by Chuck Dillon

ladle
ice-cream bar
candle
necktie
celery
artist's brush
iron
grapes
boot
radish
sailboat
tape dispenser
leaf
slice of bread
banana
glove
wrench
flag
tweezers

A Horse's Tale

Art by Scott Brooks

pennant

needle

banana

heart

ring

pliers

funnel

toothbrush

cupcake

crown

bird

hat

crescent moon

mug

thimble

balloon

lollipop

artist's brush

Sheriff Saddleback

Art by Tim Davis

pencil

toothbrush

ice-cream cone

key

crown

shoe

paper clip

heart

bell

2 birds

mallet

fish

teacup

ruler

Drumming Day

comb

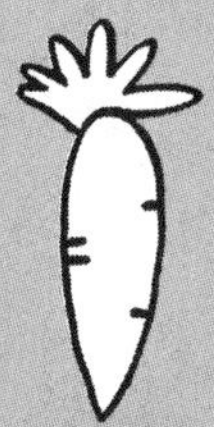

carrot

banana

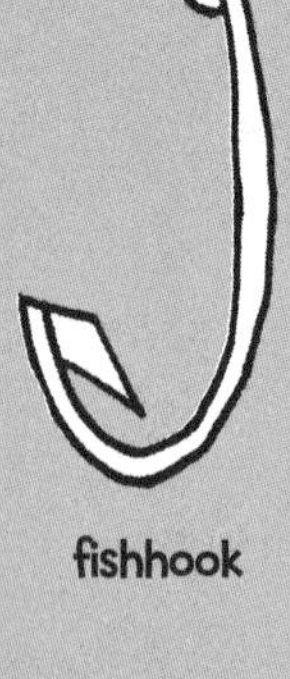

fishhook

button

top hat

cupcake

Art by Mernie Gallagher-Cole

bell

candy cane

lollipop

slice of watermelon

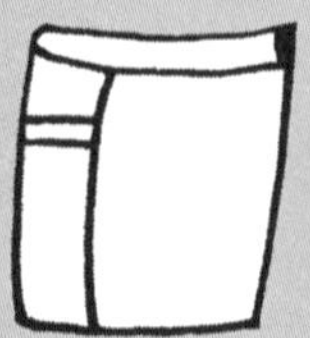

book

broccoli

mushroom

Past the Pasture

Art by Charles Jordan

artist's brush

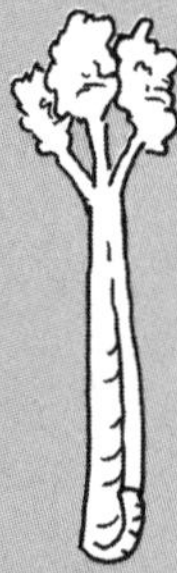

celery

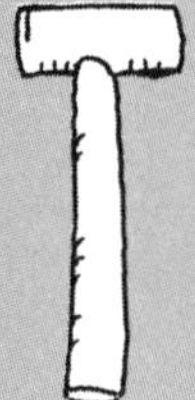

mallet

flower

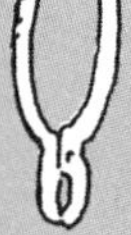

pliers

crayon

nail

musical note

pencil

slice of pie

fish

pushpin

Gallop up the Path

Art by Gay Holland

jacket

pencil

mallet

platter

grapes

funnel

shoe

rowboat

stool

wishbone

fish

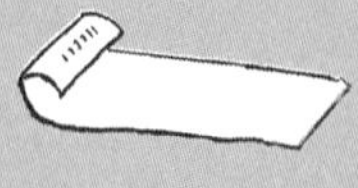

sled

sock

Horseplay

Art by Mernie Gallager-Cole

carrot

baseball bat

crescent moon

exclamation point

snake

fork

leaf

ghost

cupcake

snail

envelope

fried egg

banana

ruler

Bucking Bronco

Art by Charles Jordan

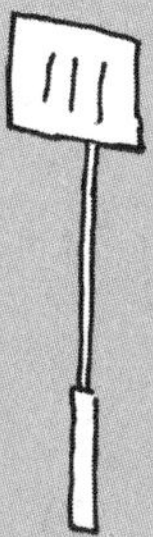
spatula

candle

golf club

slice of cake

slice of pie

magic wand

mitten

paintbrush

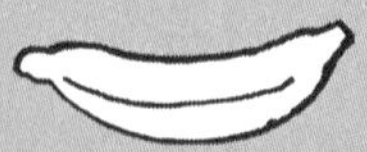
banana

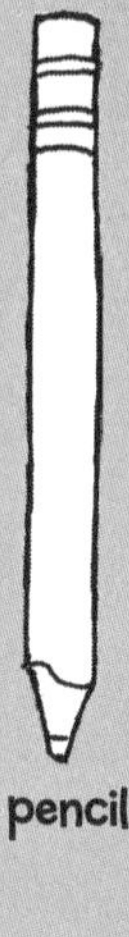
pencil

snail

flyswatter

ring

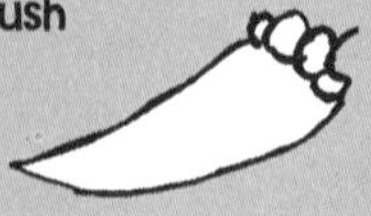
chili pepper

spool of thread

Pony-Riding Party

artist's brush

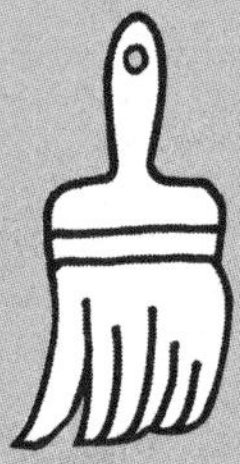
paintbrush

pencil

broccoli

lemon

carrot

shoe

open book

fish

teacup

mitten

envelope

cherries

saw

light bulb

heart

Art by Maggie Swanson

baseball bat

ice-cream cone

screwdriver

screw

key

acorn

star

can

candle

canoe

seashell

spoon

clothespin

fork

banana

slice of pizza

rabbit

ring

crown

The Reining Winner Is . . .

Art by Elizabeth Allyn

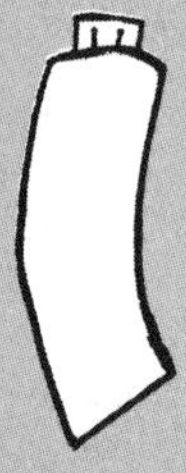
tube of toothpaste

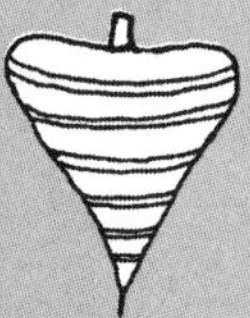
toy top

pencil

candle

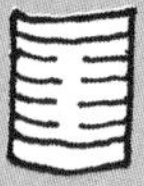
spool of thread

snake

bat

canoe

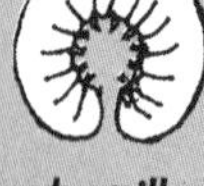
caterpillar

teacup

bowl

ring

bird

Lasso Larry
iron
scissors
eyeglasses
duck
artist's brush
heart
rabbit
key
chicken
dinosaur
baseball cap
seal
boomerang
Art by Tim Davis

Bridle Party

Art by Rich Powell

fishhook

mitten

lollipop

slice of pizza

sailboat

apple

chef's hat

cinnamon bun

crescent moon

slice of pie

banana

canoe

seashell

Grooming the Groom

Art by Laura Zarrin

slice of pizza

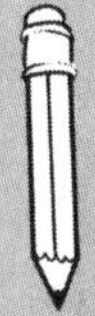

pencil

pear

magnifying glass

paper clip

belt

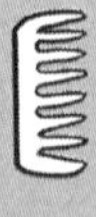

comb

arrow

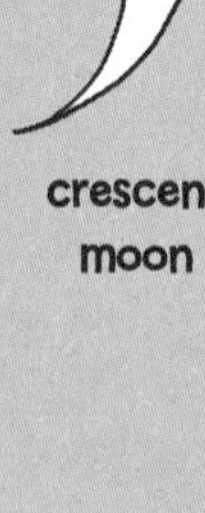

crescent moon

worm

fish

wristwatch

teacup

Full of Oats
Art by Janet Robertson
nail
cane
artist's brush
pennant
pen
chili pepper
broom
duck
mushroom
candle
necklace
worm
mitten
banana
leaf
pencil
telephone receiver
flashlight
snake

Howdy!

Art by George Wildman

artist's brush

banana

umbrella

kite

wishbone

open book

bird

fork

carrot

teacup

funnel

megaphone

sailboat

snake

slice of lemon

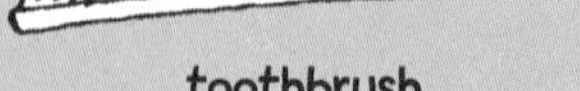

toothbrush

Pony Rides

hockey stick

hammer

broccoli

saw

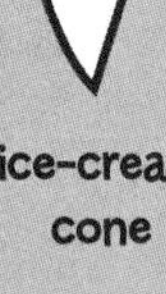

ice-cream
cone

Art by Melissa Iwai

pencil

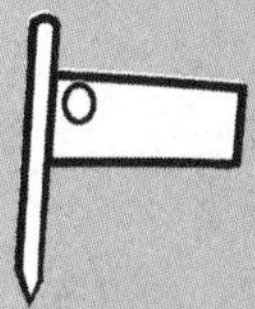

flag

wishbone

baby's bottle

crown

teacup

mitten

Horsing Around
flower
traffic light
artist's brush
pencil
pine tree
bowl
Art by Jennifer Harney
mug
wristwatch
lollipop
crown
toothbrush
musical note
mushroom
banana
whale
heart
snail
dragonfly
cupcake
handbell
candy cane
114

The Neighs Have It

Art by Gary LaCoste

hockey stick
drinking straw
ladder
candy cane
domino
toothbrush
banana
lollipop
wedge of lemon
crescent moon
shoe
worm
envelope
mushroom
golf club

The Best in Show

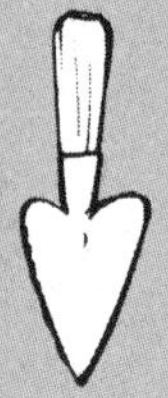

trowel

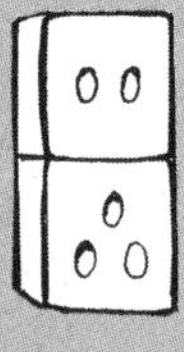

domino

scissors

safety pin

fried egg

heart

Art by Ellen Appleby

baseball bat

toothbrush

cupcake

frog

iron

football

Horse Tales

toothbrush

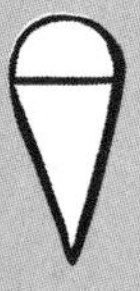
snow cone

comb

paper clip

bird

trowel

Art by Tim Davis

spoon

banana

heart

slice of pie

sailboat

fish

Paddock Pals

Art by Christine Schneider

pencil

ruler

lollipop

feather

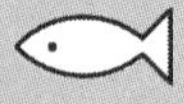
fish

banana

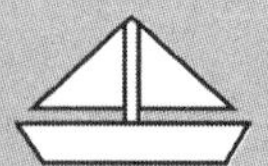
sailboat

fried egg

ring

funnel

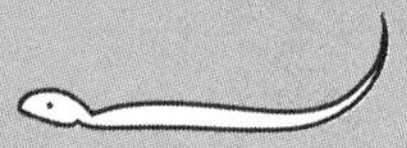
snake

nail

Crossing Ducks

Art by George Wildman

crescent moon

hairbrush

artist's brush

pennant

carrot

cupcake

shoe

fork

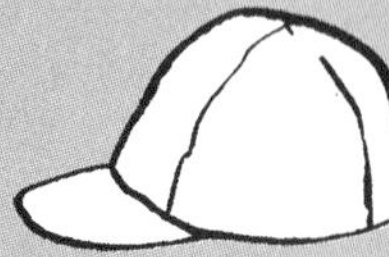

baseball cap

candle

cotton candy

ice-cream bar

Saddleback Trails

tube of toothpaste

ice-cream bar

tack

saltshaker

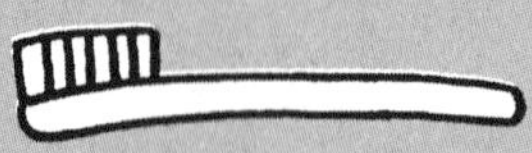

toothbrush

envelope

Art by R. Michael Palan

carrot

crayon

ring

slice of cake

teacup

trowel

The Desert's Mane Trail

bowling pin

banana

artist's brush

piece of candy

slipper

mitten

Art by Jacob Chabot

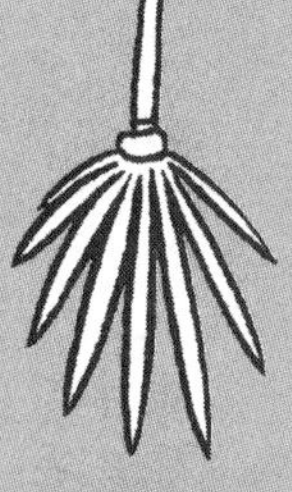

feather duster

pen

screwdriver

oar

dolphin

slice of watermelon

pie

Jumping Contest

Art by Kathy Swain-O'Brien

iron

duck

chicken

pie

ice-cream cone

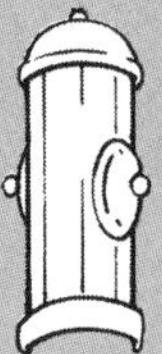
fire hydrant

hammer

envelope

ladle

piece of popcorn

rolling pin

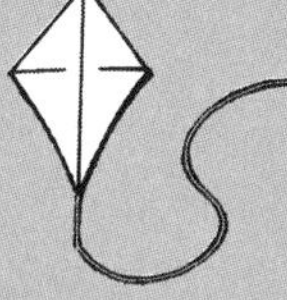
kite

dinosaur

fish

cupcake

sailboat

crown

bell

clothespin

bowling pin

Traveling with Friends

Art by Deborah Johnson

cinnamon roll

banana

ice-cream cone

paintbrush

flag

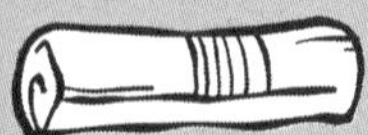

scroll

mailbox

ship

flashlight

belt

muffin

mug

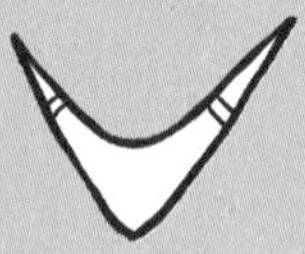

boomerang

knitted hat

caterpillar

bird

pencil

Neigh-bors

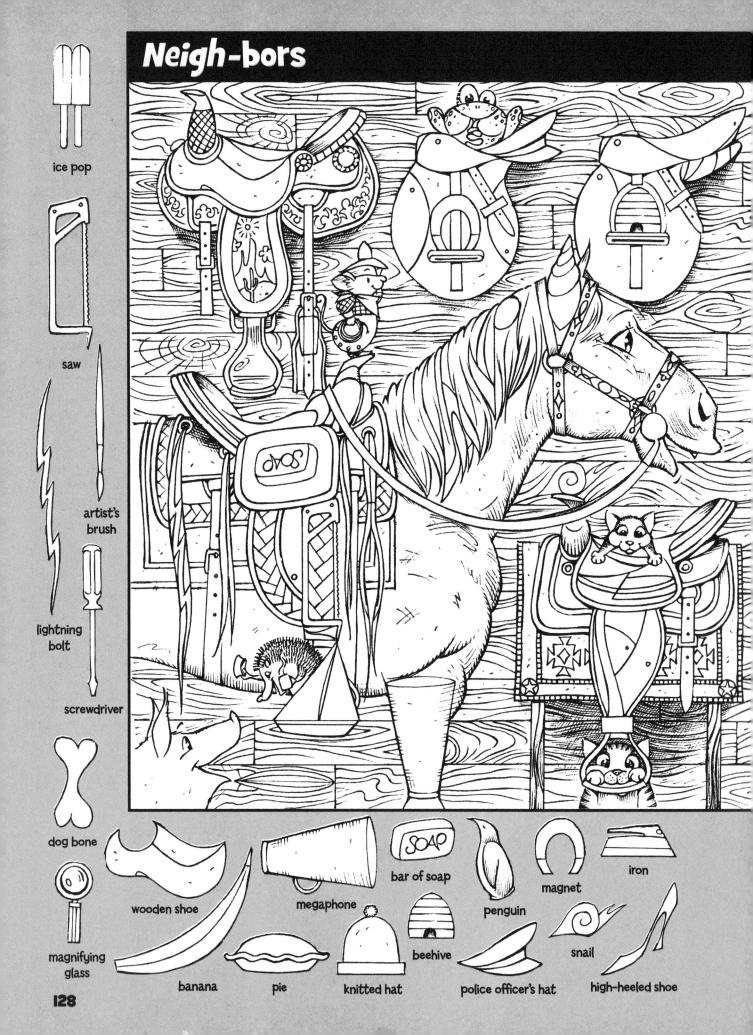

ice pop

saw

artist's brush

lightning bolt

screwdriver

dog bone

magnifying glass

wooden shoe

banana

megaphone

pie

knitted hat

bar of soap

beehive

penguin

police officer's hat

magnet

snail

iron

high-heeled shoe

ax
bicycle pump
cherry
musical note
candle
paper clip
tweezers
Art by Mark Corcoran
tape dispenser
bottle cap
bowl
slipper
wishbone
vase
butter knife
spoon
whale
sailboat
seashell
rolling pin
blimp
shark
wedge of lemon

Answers

▼Pages 4-5

▼Page 6

▼Page 7

▼Page 8

▼Page 9

▼Pages 10-11

▼Page 12

Answers

▼Page 13

▼Page 14

▼Page 15

▼Pages 16-17

▼Page 18

▼Page 19

▼Page 20

▼Page 21

Answers

▼Page 22

▼Page 23

▼Page 24

▼Page 25

▼Page 26

▼Page 27

▼Pages 28-29

▼Page 30

Answers

▼Page 31

▼Page 32

▼Page 33

▼Page 34

▼Page 35

▼Page 36

▼Page 37

▼Pages 38-39

Answers

▼Page 40

▼Page 41

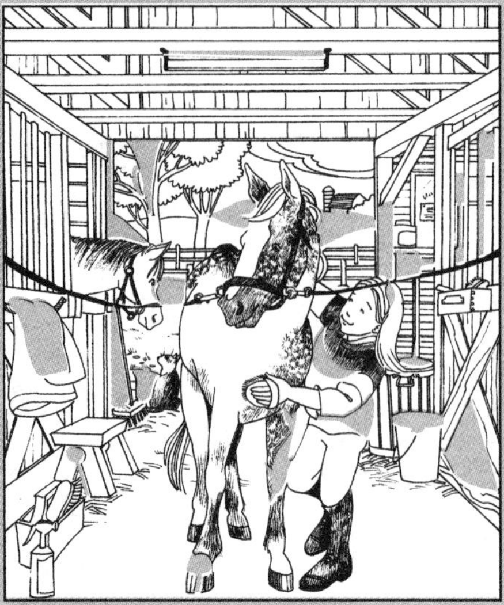

▼Page 42

▼Page 43

▼Pages 44-45

▼Page 46

▼Page 47

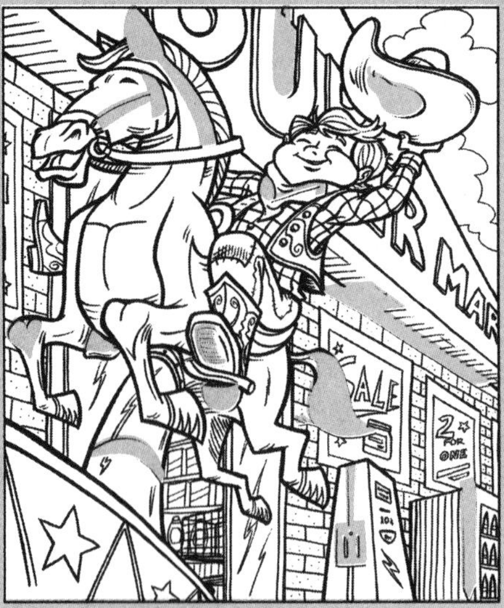

▼Page 48

▼Page 49

▼Page 50

▼Page 51

▼Pages 52-53

▼Page 54

▼Page 55

▼Page 56

▼Page 57

Answers

▼Page 58

▼Page 59

▼Page 60

▼Page 61

▼Page 62

▼Page 63

▼Pages 64-65

▼Page 66

Answers

▼Page 67

▼Page 68

▼Page 69

▼Pages 70-71

▼Page 72

▼Page 73

▼Page 74

▼Page 75

Answers

▼Pages 76-77

▼Page 78

▼Page 79

▼Page 80

▼Page 81

▼Pages 82-83

▼Page 84

▼Page 85

▼Pages 86-87

▼Page 88

▼Page 89

▼Page 90

▼Page 91

▼Pages 92-93

Answers

▼Page 94

▼Page 95

▼Page 96

▼Page 97

▼Pages 98-99

▼Page 100

▼Page 101

▼Page 102

▼Page 103

▼Pages 104-105

▼Page 106

▼Page 107

▼Page 108

▼Page 109

▼Page 110

▼Page 111

Answers

▼Pages 112-113

▼Page 114

▼Page 115

▼Pages 116-117

▼Pages 118-119

▼Page 120

▼Page 121

▼Pages 122-123

▼Pages 124-125

▼Page 126

▼Page 127

▼Pages 128-129

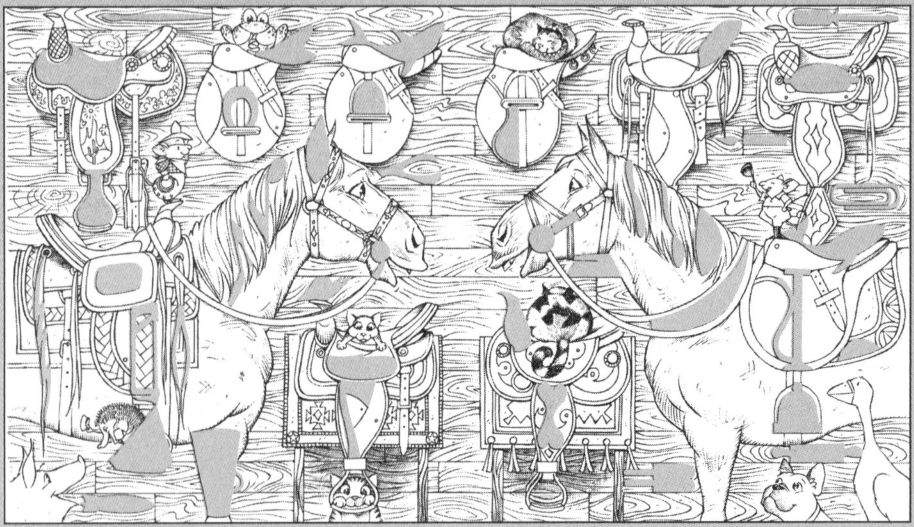

Published by Highlights for Children
P.O. Box 18201
Columbus, Ohio 43218-0201
Printed in the United States of America
ISBN: 978-1-62979-841-7

First edition
Visit our website at Highlights.com.
10 9 8 7 6 5 4 3 2 1